The seven deadly sins
of
chocolate

The seven deadly sins of chocolate

RECIPES BY LAURENT SCHOTT

PHOTOGRAPHS BY THOMAS DHELLEMMES
STYLING BY VÉRONIQUE VILLARET
EDITORIAL CONSULTANT PIERRE JASKARZEC

HACHETTE
Illustrated

The seven deadly

Sloth

• Tart à l'antillaise, 8 • Pear jam with chocolate, 10 •
• Warm chocolate fondants, 12 • Chocolate pancakes, 14 •
• Banana jam with chocolate, 16 • Floating islands, 18 •
• Bourdaloue tart, 20 •

Anger

• Red-fruit chocolate tart, 24 • Viennese chocolate cake, 26 •
• Crèmes brûlées flavoured with Earl Grey tea, 28 •
• Black Forest gateau, 30 • Spiced hot chocolate, 32 •
• Viennese chocolate sablés, 34 • Marble cake, 36 •

Lust

• Religieuses, 40 • Pears Belle-Hélène, 42 •
• Opera cakes, 44 • Raspberry chocolate tart, 46 •
• Chocolate savarins with vanilla cream, 48 •
• Chocolate mousse trilogy, 50 • Chocolate ices, 52 •

Pride

• Chocolate orange thins, 56 • Saint-Honoré, 58 •
• Profiteroles, 60 • Twelfth-Night cake, 62 •
• Chocolate macaroons, 64 • Kouglofs, 66 •
• Concorde, 68 • Mille-feuille, 70 •

sins of chocolate

Envy

Avarice

Gluttony

Secrets of the great chocolatiers

Sloth

Sloth needs no introduction since everyone has their own particular idea of 'that indolent but agreeable condition of doing nothing' (*Letters*, Pliny the Younger, AD 62–114). It may be a fat cat snoozing in the summer heat, or those Sunday mornings in winter when only the aroma of coffee drags you from your bed. According to French writer Jules Renard (1864–1910), activity thinks while sloth dreams. In fact, day-dreaming is an integral part of sloth – day-dreaming and reliving childhood memories. On the beach, during the summer holidays, worn out by a day of playing games, swimming and running wild. It is late afternoon and you're lying on the warm sand with your eyes half closed, watching your mother preparing a teatime snack. In her hand, she's holding a bar of your favourite chocolate, the one that tastes deliciously of hazelnuts – and the end of summer.

Tart à l'antillaise

This tart with its tropical flavours provides the perfect end to an exotic meal. Serve warm (by placing on a baking sheet inside the oven for just 5 minutes) so that the chocolate ganache is slightly runny, and add the finishing touch with a scoop of rum-and-raisin ice cream and a glass of old dark rum.

Serves 6

SWEET SHORTCRUST PASTRY
150 g (5 oz) unsalted butter
250 g (9 oz) plain flour
30 g (1 oz) ground almonds
90 g (3¼ oz) icing sugar
1 egg, beaten
pinch of salt

Rub the butter into the flour with your fingertips until you have a light, crumbly mixture. Add the ground almonds and icing sugar, then the egg and salt, and mix lightly to obtain a smooth, evenly textured dough. Chill in the refrigerator for several hours (12 hours if possible). Preheat the oven to 180°C (350°F), gas mark 4. Roll out the pastry to a thickness of 3 mm/⅛ inch and use to line a flan dish, 22 cm/8½ inches in diameter and 2 cm/¾ inch deep. Prick the pastry base with a fork. Bake in the preheated oven for 20–25 minutes then remove and leave to cool.

CHOCOLATE GANACHE
140 g (5 oz) best quality dark chocolate, 70% cocoa solids
175 ml (6 fl oz) double cream
40 g (1½ oz) unsalted butter

Chop the chocolate using a knife or food processor and put in a heatproof bowl. Bring the cream to the boil, pour onto the chocolate and mix until it has completely melted. Then add the butter, a piece at a time, mixing carefully to obtain a smooth, evenly textured ganache.
Spread the ganache over the cooled tart base and chill in the refrigerator for 30 minutes.

FLAMBÉED BANANAS
2 bananas
25 g (1 oz) unsalted butter
25 g (1 oz) soft brown sugar
2 tablespoons dark rum

Peel the bananas and cut into rounds. Heat the butter in a frying pan until it turns a nut-brown colour, add the bananas and fry for 1–2 minutes.
Add the sugar and rum, ignite, and leave to cool.
Arrange the bananas neatly on the chilled ganache base.

TO SERVE
Dark chocolate flakes

Just before serving, decorate the tart with a few flakes of dark chocolate.

Pear jam with chocolate

You'll need firm, juicy pears to make this jam. To test for setting, remove the pan from the heat and put a teaspoon of jam on a chilled saucer for a minute or two – a skin should form which wrinkles when pushed with the finger. If not, return the pan to the boil and test again at short intervals. For extra flavour and more visual impact, slip a piece of vanilla pod into each jar before covering. This jam is delicious with fresh crusty bread for breakfast or on plain buns and cake at teatime or for snacks. It will keep for up to a year if stored in a cool, dry place away from the light.

Makes approximately 10 x 200 g (7 oz) jars

200 g (7 oz) best quality dark chocolate,
70% cocoa solids
1 kg (2¼ lb) pears, weight when peeled and cored
800 g (1¾ lb) granulated sugar
juice of 1 lemon
2 vanilla pods, split open

Chop the chocolate using a knife or food processor. Peel and core the pears and chop finely. Place in a preserving pan with the sugar, lemon juice and vanilla pods. Bring to the boil, stirring gently, then boil rapidly until the setting point is reached, as described above. Add the chocolate, bring back to the boil and remove the vanilla pods.
Pour into sterilized jars and cover with lids while still hot. Turn the jars upside down and leave to cool.

Warm chocolate fondants

The best thing about this dessert is quite simply the soft, melting texture of the fondants. The fact that they are easy to make in no way detracts from the enjoyment. You can even freeze the uncooked fondants if you want to. They are particularly delicious served with a swathe of red fruit and pistachio ice cream. The fondant melting gently towards the pistachio ice cream, merging with the fragrance of the red fruit, is sheer heaven.

Serves 6

FONDANTS
100 g (3^1/$_2$ oz) best quality dark chocolate, 70% cocoa solids
100 g (3^1/$_2$ oz) unsalted butter, creamed
2 eggs
70 g (2^1/$_2$ oz) caster sugar
50 g (2 oz) plain flour
^{1}/$_2$ teaspoon baking powder
1^1/$_2$ tablespoons unsweetened cocoa powder

Melt the chocolate in a microwave, following the maker's instructions, or in a bowl set over a pan of barely simmering water (the bowl must not touch the water). Remove from the heat and stir in the creamed butter until it has completely melted and the two ingredients are well combined. Beat the eggs with the sugar and add to the chocolate mixture. Sift in the flour, baking powder and cocoa and mix together using a wooden spoon.
Grease 6 small, circular moulds – 6 cm/2^1/$_2$ inches in diameter and 4 cm/1^1/$_2$ inches deep – and pour in the fondant mixture. Chill in the refrigerator.

PISTACHIO ICE CREAM
500 ml (18 fl oz) milk
200 ml (7 fl oz) double cream
175 g (6 oz) caster sugar
7 egg yolks
70 g (2^1/$_2$ oz) pistachio paste

Put the milk, cream and half the sugar in a pan and bring to the boil. Beat the egg yolks in a bowl with the remaining sugar, then whisk in the hot milk and cream. Return the mixture to the pan over low heat and cook, stirring constantly, until the custard thickens and coats the back of the spoon and then pass through a fine-mesh sieve. Add the pistachio paste and mix well in. Cool in the refrigerator, stirring from time to time, and then churn in an ice-cream maker.

RASPBERRY COULIS
100 g (3^1/$_2$–4 oz) raspberries, crushed and sieved to remove the pips
2 tablespoons caster sugar
juice of 1 lemon

Mix all the ingredients together and leave to chill in the refrigerator.

TO BAKE AND ASSEMBLE THE FONDANTS
150 g (5 oz) red berry fruits (raspberries, blackberries, redcurrants, blueberries...)
icing sugar

Preheat the oven to 200°C (400°F), gas mark 6.
Bake the fondants for 7–8 minutes. They should be crisp on the outside but soft and melting on the inside.
Decorate one side of each plate with a spoonful of raspberry coulis and add a swathe of red fruit.
Turn out the fondants from the ramekins, dust with icing sugar, and place next to the coulis.
Add a scoop of pistachio ice cream to each plate and serve immediately.

Chocolate pancakes

Like traditional pancakes, chocolate pancakes lend themselves to a number of variations. They can be prepared like crêpes suzette, wrapped round a scoop of vanilla ice cream and flambéed with rum, filled with pistachio ice cream and crushed red fruit, or simply sprinkled with white sugar. Just make sure they're properly cooked, as their colour can be deceptive. You can also serve these pancakes filled and tied in bundles.

Makes about 20 pancakes

500 ml (18 fl oz) milk
80 g (2¾ oz) best quality dark chocolate, 70% cocoa solids
210 g (7½ oz) plain flour
3 tablespoons unsweetened cocoa powder
3 eggs
60 g (2¼ oz) caster sugar
pinch of salt
30 g (1 oz) unsalted butter
3 tablespoons dark rum

Warm the milk. Melt the chocolate in a microwave, following the maker's instructions, or in a bowl set over a pan of barely simmering water (the bowl must not touch the water). Stir in half the milk when the chocolate has melted.
Process the rest of the milk with the flour, cocoa, eggs, sugar and salt in an electric mixer. Melt the butter and add to the mixer, along with the rum and melted chocolate mixture, and process once more. Chill the pancake mixture in the refrigerator for 3 hours.
Cook the pancakes in a nonstick frying pan.

Banana jam with chocolate

This versatile jam is as at home on the breakfast table as it is served with chocolate macaroons and a cup of tea or coffee. It keeps perfectly well if stored in a cool, dry place away from the light. For a more intense taste, use really ripe bananas.

Makes approximately 10 x 200 g (7 oz) jars

1 kg (2¼ lb) bananas
800 g (1¾ lb) granulated sugar
juice of 1 lemon
175 g (6 oz) best quality dark chocolate,
70% cocoa solids

Peel the bananas and cut into rounds.
Place in a preserving pan with the sugar and lemon juice.
Bring gently to the boil, stirring continuously.
Chop the chocolate using a knife or food processor.
Add to the pan and bring back to the boil. Test for a set (see recipe p. 10).
Pour into jars and cover with lids while still hot.
Turn the jars upside down and leave to cool.

Floating islands

This recipe is a variation of a classic French dessert – *oeufs à la neige*. It is easy to make and guaranteed to delight chocolate lovers and gourmets alike. The chocolate crème anglaise is made with the milk used to poach the egg whites.

Serves 6

FLOATING ISLANDS
6 egg whites
100 g (3½ oz) caster sugar
600 ml (1 pint) milk

Whisk the egg whites until they form stiff peaks, gradually incorporating the sugar about half way through the process.
Heat the milk in a pan until it simmers.
Use two spoons or an ice-cream scoop to add large scoops of egg white to the milk.
Poach for 3–4 minutes, turning half way through.
Remove the 'islands' from the pan and leave to cool on a wire rack. Do not discard the milk – it can be used to make the chocolate crème anglaise.

CHOCOLATE CRÈME ANGLAISE CUSTARD
150 g (5 oz) best quality dark chocolate, 70% cocoa solids
600 ml (1 pint) milk
140 g (5 oz) caster sugar
2 vanilla pods, split open
6 egg yolks

Chop the chocolate using a knife or food processor.
Put the milk, half the sugar and the vanilla pods into a pan and bring to the boil. Remove from the heat and leave to infuse for 15 minutes.
Beat the egg yolks with the rest of the sugar in a mixing bowl.
Bring the vanilla milk back to the boil, remove the vanilla pods and pour onto the egg mixture, whisking continuously.
Return the mixture to the pan over low heat and cook, stirring constantly, until the custard thickens and coats the back of the spoon. Pour onto the chopped chocolate through a fine-mesh sieve and mix until the chocolate has melted.
Leave to cool in the refrigerator.

TO ASSEMBLE THE DESSERT
cocoa powder
1 teaspoon chopped pistachio nuts

Pour the chocolate crème anglaise into individual dishes or glass bowls and add a floating island. Dust with cocoa powder and sprinkle with a few chopped pistachio nuts.

Bourdaloue tart

The original Bourdaloue tart was invented in the early 20th century by a French pastry cook, whose shop was located on the Rue Bourdaloue, in Paris. Although you can make this version of the classic recipe using other fruit (apricots or Morello cherries are good), it is best to use fresh pears. In season, they are even tastier when poached in vanilla syrup.

Serves 6

SWEET SHORTCRUST PASTRY

150 g (5 oz) unsalted butter
250 g (9 oz) plain flour
30 g (1 oz) ground almonds
90 g (3¼ oz) icing sugar
1 egg, beaten
pinch of salt

Rub the butter into the flour with your fingertips until you have a light, crumbly mixture. Add the ground almonds and icing sugar, then the egg and salt. Mix lightly to obtain a smooth, evenly textured dough but do not overwork the pastry. Chill in the refrigerator for several hours (12 hours if you can).
Preheat the oven to 180°C (350°F), gas mark 4.
Roll out the pastry to a thickness of 3 mm/⅛ inch and use to line a flan dish, 22 cm/8½ inches in diameter and 2 cm/¾ inch deep. Prick the pastry base with a fork. Bake in the preheated oven for 10 minutes and leave to cool.

CONFECTIONERS' CUSTARD

Makes 700 g (1 lb 9 oz)

500 ml (18 fl oz) milk
125 g (4½ oz) caster sugar
1 vanilla pod, split open
4 egg yolks
40 g (1½ oz) dried milk
50 g (2 oz) unsalted butter, cut into small pieces

Put the milk, half the sugar and the vanilla pod into a pan and bring to the boil.
In a heatproof bowl beat the egg yolks with the remaining sugar until the mixture becomes lighter in colour and then add the dried milk.
Pour the boiling milk onto the beaten egg mixture, stirring continuously with a whisk. Return the mixture to the pan and continue cooking the custard for a further 2 minutes, continuously whisking briskly with an electric whisk.
Remove from the heat and add the butter, mixing well to obtain a smooth, even texture.
Turn into a dish and leave to cool. Remove the vanilla pod, cover, and chill in the refrigerator.

CHOCOLATE FRANGIPANE

85 g (3 oz) unsalted butter
85 g (3 oz) ground almonds
85 g (3 oz) caster sugar
1 egg, beaten
15 g (½ oz) cornflour
100 g (3½ oz) confectioners' custard (see recipe left)
2 tablespoons dark rum
85 g (3 oz) best quality dark chocolate, 70% solids

Cream the butter. Add the ground almonds, sugar and beaten egg, and mix well. Then stir in the cornflour, confectioners' custard and rum. Melt the chocolate in a microwave or in a bowl set over a pan of barely simmering water, add to the frangipane, and mix well. Spread the frangipane over the base of the precooked pastry case.

TO ASSEMBLE AND BAKE THE TART

6 pear halves in syrup
toasted flaked almonds (optional)

Preheat the oven to 180°C (350°F), gas mark 4.
Thinly slice the pears and arrange in concentric circles on the frangipane, pressing down lightly. Bake in the preheated oven for 25–30 minutes. Leave to cool in the flan dish for a few minutes, then remove and leave to cool on a wire rack.

Anger

The frightening thing about anger is that it has to explode before it can subside – rather like water gushing from a geyser or fountain. This is what happens when couples argue at a dinner party – a daunting experience for the other guests. The turtle doves turn into dragons. The blood rushes to their faces, their eyes flame and their hackles rise, ready to do battle. Suddenly the angry voices merge into one, crockery is smashed as dishes are used as missiles. Mouths water as the chocolate and fruit tart is reduced to crumbs. In the words of two great Romans – one a poet and satirist, the other a philosopher and statesman – anger is indeed a 'short madness' (Horace, 65 BC–8 BC) that is 'like those ruins that smash themselves on what they fall' (Seneca, 4 BC–AD 65).

Red-fruit chocolate tart

A culinary creation in red and black, in which the slightly sharp taste of the red fruit provides a perfect complement for the bittersweet dark chocolate. It is even more delicious when served slightly warm (at about 20°C/68°F). For a more innovative version of this dessert, use hulled raspberries arranged on their tips, and add a drop of balsamic vinegar to each little 'fruit cup' to intensify the flavour. Serve with a glass of port or strong, red wine.

Serves 6

SWEET SHORTCRUST PASTRY
150 g (5 oz) unsalted butter
250 g (9 oz) plain flour
30 g (1 oz) ground almonds
90 g (3¼ oz) icing sugar
1 egg, beaten
pinch of salt

Preheat the oven to 180°C (350°F), gas mark 4.
Rub the butter into the flour with your fingertips until you have a light, crumbly mixture. Add the ground almonds and icing sugar, then the egg and salt. Mix lightly to obtain a smooth evenly textured dough but do not overwork the pastry. Leave to stand for several hours (12 hours if you have the time).
Roll out the pastry to a thickness of 3 mm/⅛ inch and use to line a flan dish, 22 cm/8½ inches in diameter and 2 cm/³/4 inch deep. Prick the base with a fork.
Bake in the preheated oven for 20–25 minutes. Remove from the oven and leave to cool.

CHOCOLATE GANACHE
WITH RASPBERRIES
175 g (6 oz) best quality dark chocolate,
70% cocoa solids
125 ml (4 fl oz) double cream
60 g (2 oz) raspberries, crushed
40 g (1½ oz) unsalted butter

Chop the chocolate using a knife or food processor.
Bring the cream and crushed raspberries to the boil in separate pans and then pour onto the chocolate.
Stir until the chocolate has melted, then add the butter, piece by piece, mixing carefully to obtain a smooth, evenly textured chocolate ganache.
Spread the ganache over the cooled tart base and chill in the refrigerator for 30 minutes.

TO ASSEMBLE THE TART
175 g (6 oz) strawberries
4 tablespoons red currant jelly
100 g (3½ oz) raspberries
50 g (2 oz) redcurrants
50 g (2 oz) blackberries
50 g (2 oz) cherries, pitted – or warn your guests!
fresh mint leaves

Halve the strawberries and arrange on the tart, cut side uppermost.
Warm the jelly and brush over the strawberries. Fill the spaces with raspberries, redcurrants and blackberries, top with cherries and decorate with fresh mint leaves.

Viennese chocolate cake

This cake is a version of the famous sachertorte created at the Congress of Vienna (1814–1815) by Franz Sacher, Metternich's chief pastrycook. The original recipe for sachertorte (literally, 'Sacher's cake') remains a closely guarded secret by the Hotel Sacher, but our recipe conforms to all the traditions of Viennese patisserie – well-textured sponge, delicious cream filling and the finest quality chocolate covering. Remember to remove it from the refrigerator 3 hours before serving as the combination of chocolate ganache and apricot jam is best appreciated at room temperature.

Serves 6

SPONGE BASE

25 g (1 oz) plain flour
15 g ($^1/_2$ oz) cornflour
3 tablespoons unsweetened cocoa powder
4 egg yolks + 3 egg whites
100 g (3$^1/_2$ oz) caster sugar
40 g (1$^1/_2$ oz) unsalted butter

Preheat the oven to 180°C (350°F), gas mark 4. Grease and flour a 16-cm/6$^1/_2$-inch cake tin.
Sift the flour, cornflour and cocoa into a bowl. Beat the egg yolks with 60 g (2$^1/_4$ oz) of the sugar until they are light and frothy. Using an electric whisk, beat the egg whites until they form stiff peaks, adding the rest of the sugar half way through the process.
Melt the butter. Gently fold in a third of the egg whites to the beaten egg mixture with a metal spoon. Then add the melted butter and the sifted flour, cornflour and cocoa. Finally fold in the rest of the egg whites.
Pour the mixture into the prepared cake tin and bake in the preheated oven for about 30 minutes. Remove from the tin and leave to cool on a wire rack.
When cold, slice the cake horizontally into 3 layers of equal thickness.

CHOCOLATE GANACHE

200 g (7 oz) best quality dark chocolate, 70% cocoa solids
150 ml (5 fl oz) double cream
50 g (2 oz) unsalted butter, diced

Melt the chocolate in a microwave, following the maker's instructions, or in a bowl set over a pan of barely simmering water (the bowl must not touch the water).

Bring the cream to the boil, and pour the cream onto the melted chocolate. Mix until smooth, then add the butter, one piece at a time, mixing well to obtain a smooth, evenly textured ganache.

ASSEMBLING THE CAKE

apricot jam, warmed

Spread each of the three cake layers with a thin layer of apricot jam. Spread a third of the chocolate ganache over the jam on each layer, up to the edges, but not over. Stack the layers into a single cake. Cut a strip of baking parchment to the depth of the cake by the circumference of the cake plus an inch or two. Wrap the strip around the cake, fastening the overlap with a piece of sticky tape, to hold the layers firmly in place while chilling. Place in the refrigerator to chill for at least 5 hours.

TO ICE THE CAKE

115 g (4 oz) best quality dark chocolate, 70% cocoa solids
4 tablespoons water
2 teaspoons glycerine
85 g (3 oz) sifted icing sugar
toasted flaked nuts (optional)
Melt the chocolate with the water, beat in the glycerine and sufficient icing sugar to obtain a coating consistency. Take care that it is not too stiff to spread – nor too runny, or it will not adhere well to the cake's sides. Remove the paper strip and smooth the coating over the top and sides of the cake with a palette knife and return to the refrigerator to set. Decorate with toasted nuts, if desired.

Crèmes brûlées flavoured with Earl Grey tea

This extremely elegant dessert is served as soon as the crèmes brûlées have caramelized, so that the cold cream highlights the warm, crunchy texture of the topping. If possible, caramelize using a kitchen blowtorch rather than under the grill. Start to make the dessert the day before caramelizing so that the cream part sets well.

Serves 6

250 g (9 oz) best quality milk chocolate
200 ml (7 fl oz) milk
3–4 Earl Grey teabags
6 egg yolks
400 ml (14 fl oz) double cream
80 g (2¾ oz) soft light brown sugar

Chop the chocolate using a knife or food processor and put in a heatproof bowl. Bring the milk to the boil, add the teabags, remove from the heat, and leave to infuse for 5 minutes. Remove the teabags, pass through a fine-mesh sieve and bring back to the boil. Pour onto the chopped chocolate and whisk briskly with an electric whisk or until the chocolate has melted.

Preheat the oven to 140°C (275°F), gas mark 1.
Beat the egg yolks and add to the chocolate-and-milk mixture, then add the cream.
Divide the mixture between 6 ramekin dishes, place in a roasting pan filled with hot water half way up the ramekins and bake in the preheated oven for 30–40 minutes or until the creams have set.
Leave to chill in the refrigerator overnight, or for at least 6 hours.
Sprinkle the creams with brown sugar and caramelize with a blowtorch or under a very hot grill.
Serve immediately.

Black Forest gateau

This Black Forest gateau, inherited from the culinary tradition of Germany, doesn't give anything away – its impressive exterior conceals layers of incredibly light Genoese sponge and frothy Chantilly cream flavoured with kirsch. Just do not be too heavy handed with the kirsch if you are serving this dessert to young gourmets. This is a truly splendid dinner party dessert or a delightful, private indulgence with a cup of tea in the afternoon.

Serves 6

GENOESE CHOCOLATE SPONGE

3 eggs
100 g (3 1/2 oz) caster sugar
75 g (2 3/4 oz) plain flour
20 g (3/4 oz) cornflour
2 tablespoons unsweetened cocoa powder

Preheat the oven to 180°C (350°F), gas mark 4.
Butter and flour a 20-cm/8-inch sponge tin.
Beat the eggs and sugar together in a bowl for 5 minutes. Place the bowl over a pan of barely simmering water and continue beating until the mixture is thick and frothy. (Do not allow the bowl to touch the water or the eggs may 'scramble'.) Remove the bowl from the pan and continue beating until the mixture is completely cold.
Sift the flour, cornflour and cocoa into a bowl and then carefully stir into the egg mixture with a wooden spoon. Pour the mixture into the sponge tin and bake in the preheated oven for about 30 minutes. Check that the sponge is cooked by inserting the blade of a knife into the middle – it should come out clean. Turn the sponge out onto a wire rack and leave to cool.

CHANTILLY CREAM WITH KIRSCH

400 ml (14 fl oz) whipping cream
35 g (1 1/4 oz) caster sugar
2 tablespoons kirsch

Beat the cream and sugar until you have a firm Chantilly cream (the texture of a firm mousse). Add the kirsch and mix carefully.
Chill in the refrigerator.

SYRUP

Makes 900 ml (1 1/2 pints)
500 ml (18 fl oz) water
675 g (1 1/2 lb) caster sugar

Mix the water and sugar in a pan and bring to the boil. Leave to cool and use when it has reached a temperature of 30°C/86°F. The syrup can be made in advance and reheated.

TO ASSEMBLE THE GATEAU

150 ml (1/4 pint syrup) at 30°C/86°F (see recipe above)
4 tablespoons kirsch
400 g (14 oz) canned or bottled cherries
100 g (3 1/2 oz) bar best quality dark chocolate, 70% cocoa solids
unsweetened cocoa powder

Mix the syrup with the kirsch and drain the cherries. Slice the cake horizontally into 3 equal layers. Drizzle one of the layers with a third of the kirsch-syrup, spread with a layer (1 cm/1/2 inch) of Chantilly cream and dot with cherries (reserving some for decoration). Repeat with the second layer and place on top of the first. Drizzle the third layer with the rest of the kirsch-syrup and place on top of the other two.
Completely cover the gateau with the remaining Chantilly cream, smoothing the surface with a palette knife. Cut shavings from the bar of chocolate with a potato peeler and use them to decorate the gateau, pressing lightly into the cream. Dust with cocoa powder and decorate with cherries.
Chill in the refrigerator until ready to serve.

Spiced
hot chocolate

With its smooth, creamy texture and delicate flavour, every mouthful of this hot-chocolate drink is a sheer pleasure that can be enjoyed at any time of the day. For those with a particularly sweet tooth, it would simply not be complete without a swirl of Chantilly cream on top, sprinkled with cocoa powder.

Serves 4

250 g (9 oz) best quality dark chocolate, 70% cocoa solids
900 ml (1½ pints) milk
200 ml (7 fl oz) whipping cream
2 cinnamon sticks
1 vanilla pod, split open
4 tablespoons soft brown sugar

Chop the chocolate very finely using a knife or food processor.
Put the milk, cream, cinnamon sticks and vanilla pod in a pan and bring to the boil. Remove from the heat, leave to infuse for 10 minutes and then bring back to the boil. Remove the cinnamon sticks and vanilla pod and pour the milk carefully onto the chocolate, beating briskly. Stir in the sugar and serve piping hot.

Viennese chocolate sablés

What could be better for satisfying that sudden urge for 'something sweet' than these delicate cookies with their light, crumbly texture? They are delicious with coffee and can be stored in an airtight box, in a cool dry place.

Makes 30–35 small sablés

175 g (6 oz) unsalted butter
60 g (2¹/4 oz) icing sugar, plus extra for decoration
1 egg white
185 g (6¹/4 oz) plain flour
3 tablespoons unsweetened cocoa powder
pinch of salt

Preheat the oven to 190°C (375°F), gas mark 5. Cover a baking sheet with nonstick baking parchment. Soften the butter and process in an electric mixer with the icing sugar, egg white, flour, cocoa and salt to obtain a smooth, even texture.
Using a piping bag with a fluted nozzle, pipe the mixture onto the baking sheet. Bake in the preheated oven for 15–20 minutes. Leave to cool on the sheet for a few minutes before transferring to a wire rack and dust with icing sugar.

Marble cake

This easy-to-make cake is ideal for brightening up a picnic basket or taking on a journey. For added flavour, the recipe uses small pieces of candied orange but you can replace the orange with other candied fruits or dried fruit soaked in rum. Whatever you use, remember to take all the ingredients out of the refrigerator a few hours before making the cake – that way the mixture will be smooth and pliable.

Serves 6–8

90 g (3¼ oz) candied oranges, or just the peel, diced
4 tablespoons Grand Marnier
175 g (6 oz) unsalted butter
175 g (6 oz) caster sugar
3 eggs
175 g (6 oz) plain flour
1 teaspoon baking powder
3½ tablespoons unsweetened cocoa powder

Preheat the oven to 200°C (400°F), Gas Mark 6.
Butter and flour an 18-cm/7-inch cake tin.
Place the pieces of candied orange in a bowl and pour over 2 tablespoons of the Grand Marnier. Set aside and leave to soak.

Process the butter, sugar, eggs, flour and baking powder in an electric mixer until you obtain a smooth, pliable mixture. Add the candied oranges and process for another 5 seconds. Divide the mixture in half, add the cocoa to one half and mix well.
Put alternate, irregular layers of the two cake mixtures into the tin to create a marbled effect.
Bake in the preheated oven for 10 minutes and then reduce to 180°C (350°F), gas mark 4, for 45–50 minutes. Check that the cake is cooked by inserting the blade of a knife into the centre. When it comes out dry, remove the cake from the oven. Turn out onto a wire rack, place a plate underneath the rack to catch the drips, and drizzle the cake with the rest of the Grand Marnier. Leave to cool completely.

Lust

Lips caught in the act of a melting kiss, desire aroused by a caress – the sensuality of lovers has all the insatiable ardour of excessive indulgence. Moreover, a hot chocolate or a piece of something sweet can only serve to sweeten pleasures, bring fantasies to the boil and intoxicate the mind with their heady aromas. In the words of the Marquis de Sade:

> 'I know of nothing that stimulates my stomach and excites my mind more voluptuously than the aromas of these delicious dishes as they caress the imagination and arouse feelings of desire.' (*La Nouvelle Justine ou les Malheurs de la Vertu*, 1797)

Religieuses

Chocolate religieuses are a must when it comes to the sin of indulgence and French patisserie. To appreciate fully the smooth creaminess of the chocolate filling and the lightly melting texture of the choux pastry, leave at room temperature for a few minutes before serving. The name comes from the colour of the icing, which resembles a nun's habit.

Makes 6 religieuses

CHOUX PASTRY
125 ml (4 fl oz) water
125 ml (4 fl oz) milk
125 g (4½ oz) unsalted butter, cut into small pieces
½ teaspoon salt
1 teaspoon caster sugar
165 g (5½ oz) plain flour
5 eggs

Mix the water, milk, butter, salt and sugar together in a pan and bring to the boil for 1 minute, stirring. Remove the pan from the heat and add the flour in one go. Beat with a wooden spoon for about 2 minutes until the dough forms a smooth, thick paste. Remove from the heat, transfer to a bowl and add the eggs one at a time, making sure you stir each one in before adding the next.
Preheat the oven to 190°C (375°F), gas mark 5.
Cover a baking sheet with nonstick baking parchment, and, using a piping bag, pipe 6 small choux (about the size of a walnut) for the 'heads', and 6 large choux (about 5–6 cm/2–2½ inches in diameter) for the 'bodies' of the religieuses.
Bake in the preheated oven for about 20 minutes for the small choux and 35 minutes for the larger ones. Remove from the baking sheet and leave to cool on a wire rack.

CHOCOLATE CONFECTIONERS' CUSTARD
100 g (3½ oz) best quality dark chocolate, 70% cocoa solids
500 g (1 lb 2 oz) confectioners' custard (see recipe p. 20)
4 tablespoons whipping cream

Melt the chocolate in a microwave, following the maker's instructions, or in a bowl set over a pan of barely simmering water (the bowl must not touch the water). Warm the confectioners' custard and add the chocolate to the custard. Add the whipping cream and mix well to obtain a smooth, creamy texture.
Make a small hole in the base of each choux and, using a piping bag, fill with the custard.

CHOCOLATE ICING
(Makes about 900g (2 lb) icing)
6 gelatine leaves (for powdered gelatine: use 1½ x 11 g sachets and follow the maker's instructions for dissolving)
4 tablespoons water
450 g (1 lb) caster sugar
150 g (5 oz) unsweetened cocoa powder
300 ml (½ pint) whipping cream

Soak the gelatine leaves in cold water. Mix the measured water, sugar, cocoa and cream in a pan and bring to the boil. Reduce over low heat for 5 minutes, stirring continuously.
Squeeze the water from the gelatine and add the leaves to the pan. (If using powdered gelatine add the dissolved powder to the pan) Mix well, remove from the heat, and leave to cool. The icing is ready to use when it has reached a temperature of 30–35°C/86–95°F.

TO ASSEMBLE THE RELIGEUSES
300 g (10½ oz) chocolate icing (see recipe above)

Warm the icing in the microwave (or a very cool oven) to 30–35°C/86–95°F. Dip the top half of each choux into the icing, turn the right way up and leave to cool. Place the small choux ('heads') on the larger ones ('bodies') while the icing is still soft.

Pears Belle-Hélène

Pears poached in syrup, vanilla ice cream and hot chocolate sauce – how could anyone resist this delicious dessert? To allow the flavours to develop fully, leave the vanilla pods to infuse overnight in the milk to be used for making the ice cream. If you prefer, you can make the dessert with chocolate ice cream instead of vanilla.

Serves 6

PEARS POACHED IN VANILLA SYRUP
6 pears
juice of 1 lemon
1 litre (1³/4 pints) water
400 g (14 oz) caster sugar
1 vanilla pod, split open

Peel and halve the pears, and remove the core. Dip quickly in the lemon juice to prevent them discolouring Put the water, sugar and vanilla pod into a pan and bring to the boil.
Add the pears to the syrup and simmer gently over low heat for 15–20 minutes or until cooked through but do not let them overcook – they should remain slightly firm. Leave to cool in the syrup.

VANILLA ICE CREAM
500 ml (18 fl oz) milk
200 ml (7 fl oz) whipping cream
175 g (6 oz) caster sugar
2 vanilla pods, split open
7 egg yolks

Put the milk, cream, half the sugar and the vanilla pods into a saucepan and bring to the boil. Remove from the heat and leave to infuse for 20 minutes.
Beat the egg yolks with the rest of the sugar until the mixture lightens in colour.
Remove the vanilla pods and pour the hot milk onto the egg mixture, whisking continuously.
Return the mixture to the pan and stir over low heat until the custard thickens and coats the back of a spoon then pass through a fine-mesh sieve.
Cool in the refrigerator, stirring from time to time, and then churn in an ice-cream maker.

CHOCOLATE SAUCE
125 g (4 oz) best quality dark chocolate, 70% cocoa solids
100 ml (3¹/2 fl oz) milk
4 tablespoons whipping cream
2 tablespoons caster sugar
³/4 tablespoon unsalted butter, cut into small pieces

Chop the chocolate using a knife or food processor and place in a heatproof bowl.
Put the milk, cream and sugar into a pan and bring to the boil. Pour onto the chopped chocolate, whisking briskly. Add the butter piece by piece and mix to a smooth, shiny sauce.

TO SERVE
Put 2 scoops of ice cream into individual dishes or glass bowls, top with 2 pear halves and cover with hot chocolate sauce. Serve immediately.

Opera cakes

These square, iced chocolate cakes are proof –if there was ever any doubt – that French patisserie is a form of alchemy. Exact quantities, cooking times and temperatures must be rigorously observed, and you would be well advised to use a jam thermometer when making the meringue. Opera cakes, which can be frozen before they are iced, are delicious with a glass of Cognac or a good-quality filter coffee.

Makes 12 portions

GIOCONDA SPONGE
190 g (6³/4 oz) icing sugar
190 g (6³/4 oz) ground almonds
5 eggs + 5 egg whites
40 g (1¹/2 oz) unsalted butter
25 g (1 oz) caster sugar
50 g (1³/4 oz) plain flour

Preheat the oven to 230°C (450°F), gas mark 8. Lightly butter the sides of 3 Swiss roll tins and line the bases with baking parchment.
Using an electric whisk, beat the icing sugar, almonds and 3 of the whole eggs in a basin for 5 minutes.
Add the 2 remaining eggs, one at a time, and beat for a further 5 minutes. Melt the butter in a pan and whisk in a little of the beaten egg mixture. Whisk the egg whites with the caster sugar to stiff peaks, add to the beaten egg mixture and stir gently. Then add the flour and melted butter. Divide the mixture evenly between the prepared tins and smooth with a palette knife.
Bake in the preheated oven for 5–7 minutes; the sponge should remain springy to the touch. Turn out onto a wire rack, remove the paper, and leave to cool.

COFFEE BUTTER CREAM
4 egg yolks + 2 egg whites
250 g (9 oz) caster sugar
100 ml (3¹/2 fl oz) milk
2 tablespoons water
400 g (14 oz) unsalted butter
2 tablespoons liquid coffee extract

First make a crème anglaise custard by beating the egg yolks in a heatproof bowl with 125 g (4 oz) of the sugar. Bring the milk to the boil and pour onto the beaten egg mixture, stirring continuously. Return the mixture to the pan and stir over low heat, until it thickens and coats the back of a spoon, then pass through a fine-mesh sieve and leave to cool.
Prepare an Italian meringue by heating the remaining sugar and measured water to 121°C/250°F. Using an electric whisk, beat the egg whites to stiff peaks, then carefully add the hot sugar syrup. Continue to whisk until the meringue is cool.
Using a clean whisk, cream the butter and then add the custard, coffee extract and meringue. Stir gently to give the butter cream a smooth, even texture.

CHOCOLATE GANACHE
175 g (6 oz) best quality dark chocolate, 70% cocoa solids
125 ml (4 fl oz) milk
4 tablespoons double cream
35 g (1¹/4 oz) unsalted butter, cut into small pieces

Chop the chocolate with a knife and place in a heat-proof bowl. Pour the milk and cream into a pan, bring to the boil and pour onto the chopped chocolate. Mix until smooth and then add the butter, piece by piece, stirring carefully to obtain a smooth, shiny ganache.

COFFEE SYRUP
200 ml (7 fl oz) syrup at 30°C/86°F (see recipe p. 30)
160 ml (5¹/2 fl oz) water
1 tablespoon liquid coffee extract

Mix all the ingredients together.

TO ASSEMBLE THE CAKE
Place a layer of sponge on a baking sheet, drizzle with a third of the coffee syrup and spread evenly with half the coffee butter cream. Cover with the second layer of sponge, press down gently to make a good contact but not to allow the butter cream to ooze out. Drizzle with another third of the coffee syrup, and spread this second layer with chocolate ganache. Cover with the third layer of sponge, pressing as before, drizzle with the remaining coffee syrup, and spread with the rest of the butter cream. Chill in the refrigerator for 3 hours.

TO ICE THE CAKE
115 g (4 oz) best quality dark chocolate, 70% cocoa solids
4 tablespoons water
2 teaspoons glycerine
85 g (3 oz) sifted icing sugar

Melt the chocolate with the water. Beat in the glycerine and sufficient icing sugar to achieve a coating consistency, taking care that it is not too stiff. With a palette knife, spread the icing evenly over the surface of the cake only. Leave the icing to set, trim the sides with a sharp knife and then cut into portions.

Raspberry chocolate tart

You'll just love this chocolate tart with its contrasting flavours, textures and colours. The combination of raspberries and chocolate, and the creamy smoothness of the confectioners' custard, offset the crunchiness of the peanut brittle in this deliciously extravagant creation. If you prefer, you can make individual tartlets. A glass of port or strong red wine provides the perfect accompaniment for this delicious dessert.

Serves 6

SWEET SHORTCRUST PASTRY

150 g (5 oz) unsalted butter
250 g (9 oz) plain flour
30 g (1 oz) ground almonds
90 g (3^1/4 oz) icing sugar
1 egg, beaten
pinch of salt

Rub the butter into the flour with your fingertips until you have a light, crumbly mixture. Add the ground almonds and icing sugar, then the egg and salt, and mix lightly to obtain a smooth, evenly textured dough. Chill in the refrigerator for several hours (12 hours if possible).
Preheat the oven to 180°C (350°F), gas mark 4.
Roll out the pastry to a thickness of 3 mm/^{1}/8 inch and use to line a flan dish, 22 cm/8^1/2 inches in diameter and 2 cm/^{3}/4 inch deep. Prick the pastry base with a fork. Bake in the preheated oven for 20–25 minutes then remove and leave to cool.

PEANUT BRITTLE

125 g (4 oz) peanuts (shelled weight)
100g (3^1/2 oz) caster sugar
200 ml (7 fl oz) water
pinch of salt

Roast the peanuts in a preheated oven at 190°C (375°F), gas mark 5 for 5–10 minutes.
Put the sugar and water in a pan and cook over medium heat, stirring continuously, to obtain a caramel. Add the peanuts and salt, stirring well in so that the nuts are coated with caramel.
Turn out onto a baking tray and leave to cool.
Crush to make the peanut brittle.

CHOCOLATE CONFECTIONERS' CUSTARD

60 g (2^1/4 oz) best quality dark chocolate, 70% cocoa solids
300 g (10^1/2 oz) confectioners' custard (see recipe p. 20)
2 tablespoons whipping cream

Melt the chocolate in a microwave, following the maker's instructions, or in a bowl set over a pan of barely simmering water (the bowl must not touch the water). Warm the confectioners' custard and stir in the chocolate. Add the whipping cream and mix well to obtain a smooth, creamy texture.

TO ASSEMBLE THE TART

peanut brittle (see recipe left)
200 g (7 oz) fresh raspberries

Add all but 1–2 tablespoons of the peanut brittle to the chocolate confectioners' custard and then use to line the bottom of the cooked pastry case. Cover with a tightly packed layer of raspberries.
Serve the tart sprinkled with the remaining crushed peanut brittle.

Chocolate savarins with vanilla cream

As is so often the case in patisserie, the flavour of the vanilla releases the full aroma of the chocolate. So make the most of your vanilla by using a small knife to scrape out the seeds contained in the pods. What is more, a savarin can be easily frozen once it has been cooked and soaked with syrup. In this recipe, the savarin sponge rings are drizzled with rum and covered with an apricot glaze, while the centre is filled with vanilla cream.

Makes 2 savarins (12 servings)

CHOCOLATE SAVARIN MIXTURE
200 g (7 oz) plain flour
3 1/2 tablespoons unsweetened cocoa powder
1 1/2 tablespoons caster sugar
pinch of salt
5 g (1/4 oz) dried yeast
3 eggs
4 tablespoons milk
75 g (2 3/4 oz) unsalted butter
70 g (2 1/2 oz) chocolate chips

Using a food processor, mix together the flour, cocoa, sugar, salt, yeast, eggs and milk, then knead the dough rapidly for 5 minutes using the hook attachment. Alternatively, mix well in a bowl and knead by hand. Melt the butter and add to the dough, kneading at a moderate speed for another 2 minutes. Carefully mix in the chocolate chips.
Grease two 18-cm/7-inch savarin moulds and three-quarters fill with dough. Leave the dough to rise until it is level with the top of the moulds.
Preheated the oven to 190°C (375°F), gas mark 5 and bake the savarins for about 20 minutes. Turn out of the moulds and leave to cool on a wire rack.

VANILLA CREAM
1 vanilla pod, split open
500 ml (18 fl oz) whipping cream
4 tablespoons caster sugar

Leave the vanilla pod to infuse in the cream overnight. The next day, remove the pod and, using an electric whisk, beat the cream with the sugar until you have a firm Chantilly cream (the texture of a firm mousse). Chill in the refrigerator.

SAVARIN SYRUP
1 litre (1 3/4 pints) water
500 g (1 lb 2 oz) caster sugar
1 vanilla pod, split open
2 cinnamon sticks
2 star anise flowers
1 orange, quartered
1 lemon, quartered
150 ml (5 fl oz) dark rum

Put the water, sugar, vanilla pod, spices, and orange and lemon quarters into a pan and bring to the boil. Remove from the heat and leave to infuse for around 20 minutes. Pass through a fine-mesh sieve and stir in the rum.

TO ASSEMBLE THE SAVARINS
chocolate shavings
150 ml (5 fl oz) dark rum
150 g (5 oz) apricot jam

Stand the savarins in a shallow dish to soak in the warm syrup until they are soft and the syrup has soaked through to the centre. Leave to drain on a wire rack for 5 minutes, with a plate underneath to catch the drips, while you warm the apricot jam.
Drizzle the savarins with rum and brush with the warm jam. Fill the centre of the savarins with vanilla cream rosettes, using a piping bag with a fluted nozzle. Decorate with chocolate shavings and chill in the refrigerator until ready to serve.

Chocolate mousse trilogy

This recipe not only looks and tastes delicious but is also extremely easy to make. These three chocolate mousses in individual glasses add an attractive and original touch to any dessert buffet or the end of a meal. The contrasting colours and flavours of the chocolate mousses and fruit coulis combine to create a feast for the eyes as well as the taste buds.

Serves 6

FRUIT COULIS

ORANGE COULIS
1 gelatine leaf (^{1}/$_2$ teaspoon powdered gelatine)
150 ml (5 fl oz) fresh orange juice, strained
40 g (1^1/$_2$ oz) caster sugar

PASSION FRUIT COULIS
1 gelatine leaf (^{1}/$_2$ teaspoon powdered gelatine)
150 g (5 oz) crushed passion fruit (about 6–8 fruits, depending on size), save a few seeds for decoration
3 tablespoons caster sugar

RASPBERRY COULIS
1 gelatine leaf (^{1}/$_2$ teaspoon powdered gelatine)
150 g (5 oz) crushed raspberries, plus a few whole raspberries for decoration
2 tablespoons caster sugar
fresh mint leaves (optional)

You'll need 18 small tequila glasses or tumblers (6 for each coulis).
Soften the gelatine leaves by soaking in cold water for 5 minutes then squeeze out by hand. (If using powdered gelatine, follow the maker's instructions for dissolving.) In separate small pans heat the crushed fruit (or juice), caster sugar and gelatine (leaves or dissolved powder). Mix well, and leave to cool slightly. Divide each fruit coulis between 6 of the glasses while still warm, then chill in the refrigerator for 2 hours.

CHOCOLATE CREAM MOUSSES

WHITE CHOCOLATE MOUSSE
100 g (3^1/$_2$ oz) white chocolate
250 ml (9 fl oz) whipping cream

MILK CHOCOLATE MOUSSE
125 g (4^1/$_2$ oz) milk chocolate
250 ml (9 fl oz) whipping cream

DARK CHOCOLATE MOUSSE
125 g (4^1/$_2$ oz) best quality dark chocolate, 70% cocoa solids
250 ml (9 fl oz) whipping cream

Each of the three chocolate mousses is made in the same way.
Melt the chocolate in a microwave, following the maker's instructions, or in a bowl set over a pan of barely simmering water (the bowl must not touch the water).
Using an electric whisk, whip the cream to a soft consistency – it should not be too stiff.
Add a third of the whipped cream to the chocolate and whisk to obtain a smooth, even texture. Then add the remaining cream, stirring in gently with a wooden spoon.
Divide the chocolate cream mousses between the glasses containing the fruit coulis as follows:
• orange coulis and white chocolate mousse
• passion fruit coulis and milk chocolate mousse
• raspberry coulis and dark chocolate mousse
Chill in the refrigerator.

TO FINISH
18 pieces candied orange peel
passion fruit seeds
fresh raspberries
fresh mint leaves

Decorate each of the orange and white chocolate mousses with 3 pieces of candied orange peel; the passion fruit and milk chocolate mousses with a few passion fruit seeds; and the raspberry and dark chocolate mousses with one or two raspberries and a mint leaf.
Serve the chocolate mousse trilogies grouped together on individual rectangular dishes.

Chocolate ices

These ice creams are even more delicious if eaten as soon as they come out of the ice-cream maker – this is when they are at their smoothest and creamiest. This is also the best time to add chocolate shavings, roughly chopped cookies, or caramelized nuts.

Each flavour serves 6

DARK CHOCOLATE ICE CREAM
150 g (5 oz) best quality dark chocolate,
70% cocoa solids
500 ml (17 fl oz) milk
100 ml (3½ fl oz) whipping cream
150 g (5 oz) caster sugar
5 egg yolks

MILK CHOCOLATE ICE CREAM
200 g (7 oz) milk chocolate
500 ml (18 fl oz) milk
100 ml (3½ fl oz) whipping cream
2 tablespoons caster sugar
5 egg yolks

FOR EACH FLAVOUR
Chop the chocolate using a knife or food processor and put into a heatproof bowl.
Put the milk, cream and half the sugar in a pan and bring to the boil.
Beat the egg yolks in a heatproof basin with the rest of the sugar until the mixture lightens in colour, then whisk in the boiling milk.
Return the mixture to the pan and stir over low heat until it thickens and coats the back of a spoon. Pour over the chopped chocolate and mix until all the chocolate has melted.
Leave to cool in the refrigerator, stirring from time to time, and then churn in an ice-cream maker.

Pride

Profiteroles, macaroons and a Saint-Honoré – it was a birthday tea straight out of Ali Baba's cave. The mother looked indulgently at her child: 'Don't be so greedy, you won't want any supper.' But the child knew better and proudly promised to amaze his mother at the dinner table. But that evening, the arrogant little boy couldn't eat a thing – not even a few cake crumbs – and fell asleep dreaming of his favourite book:

"'*There!*' cried Mr Wonka, dancing up and down and pointing his gold-topped cane at the great brown river. 'It's all chocolate! Every drop of that river is hot melted chocolate of the finest quality. The *very* finest quality. There's enough chocolate in there to fill *every* bathtub in the *entire* country!'" (*Charlie and the Chocolate Factory*, Roald Dahl)

Chocolate orange thins

These crisp almond-flavoured petit fours are delicious with coffee or ice cream. Their French name (*tuiles*) derives from the fact that they are shaped like curved roofing tiles. Keep them crisp by storing in an airtight container in a cool, dry place.

Makes 40–45 thins

50 g (2 oz) unsalted butter
grated rind of 1 orange
3 tablespoons unsweetened cocoa powder
5 g (5 oz) caster sugar
2 eggs, beaten
150 g (5 oz) chopped almonds
1¹/2 tablespoons cornflour

Melt the butter and grate the orange rind.
Using a wooden spoon, mix all the ingredients together in a bowl until you have a smooth, evenly textured dough. Chill in the refrigerator for 1 hour.
Preheat the oven to 180°C (350°F), gas mark 4.
Put small pieces of dough onto baking sheet lined with nonstick baking parchment and use a spoon to flatten the pieces into rounds, making them as thin as possible. Bake in the preheated oven until they turn a slightly darker colour – keep a close watch.
Take them out of the oven and remove one at a time from the baking sheet, quickly shaping them into a 'tile' by laying them across a rolling pin while still hot. Store in an airtight container in a cool, dry place.

Saint-Honoré

This classic French – and more particularly Parisian – patisserie is thought to have been created by a pastrycook in the Rue Saint-Honoré in Paris. It takes patience and skill to make and is best served warm when the light, creamy texture can be fully appreciated.

Serves 6

SHORTCRUST PASTRY
(Makes 600 g (1 lb 5 oz) pastry)
250 g (9 oz) plain flour
80 g (2³/4 oz) cornflour
175 g (6 oz) unsalted butter, cut into small pieces
1 egg yolk
chilled water
pinch of salt

Sift together the flour, salt and cornflour, then rub in the butter with your fingertips until you have a light, crumbly mixture. Add the egg yolk and mix lightly, adding just sufficient water to obtain a smooth, even dough, but do not overwork the pastry.
Wrap in clingfilm and chill in the refrigerator.
Using 150 g (5 oz) shortcrust pastry from the above recipe (you can freeze the rest), roll out to a thickness of 3 mm/¹/8 inch, and cut a disc 20 cm/8 inches in diameter. Place on a baking sheet lined with nonstick baking parchment and prick all over with a fork.
Chill in the refrigerator.

CHOUX PASTRY
125 ml (4 fl oz) milk
125 ml (4 fl oz) water
125 g (4¹/2 oz) unsalted butter, cut into small pieces
1 teaspoon salt
1 teaspoon caster sugar
165 g (5¹/2 oz) plain flour
5 eggs

Mix the milk, water, butter, salt and sugar in a saucepan and bring to the boil. Add the flour in one go and stir in with a wooden spoon for about 2 minutes. Remove from the heat and add the eggs one at a time, stirring each one well in.
Preheat the oven to 200°C (400°F), gas mark 6.
Using a piping bag with a 14-mm/⁵/8-inch nozzle, pipe two 'crowns' of choux pastry around the pastry disc – the first 3 mm/¹/8 inch from the edge and the second in the centre. Change to a 10-mm/³/8-inch nozzle and pipe 15 small balls of choux pastry (about the size of a walnut) onto a separate baking sheet lined with baking parchment. Bake separately in the preheated oven for 20–25 minutes for the small balls and 25–30 minutes for the base – making sure you do not open the oven door while they are cooking. Remove from the baking sheet and leave to cool on a wire rack.

CHOCOLATE CONFECTIONERS' CUSTARD
60 g (2¹/4 oz) best quality dark chocolate, 70% cocoa solids
300 g (10¹/2 oz) confectioner's custard (see recipe p. 20)
2 tablespoons whipping cream

Melt the chocolate in a microwave, following maker's instructions, or in a bowl set over a pan of barely simmering water (the bowl must not touch the water). Warm the custard, and add the melted chocolate then the whipping cream, mixing in well. Using a piping bag, fill the little choux and 'crowns' with the custard.

CARAMEL
200 g (7 oz) caster sugar
4 tablespoons water

Heat the sugar and water to 150–155°C/302–311°F until it turns pale caramel. Plunge the base of the pan into cold water to stop it cooking. Dip the top third of each small ball into the caramel and place caramel-side down on a baking sheet lined with nonstick baking parchment. Let harden for 3–4 minutes, then arrange on the outer crown of choux, using a little caramel to hold in place.

DARK CHOCOLATE CREAM
150 g (5 oz) best quality dark chocolate, 70% cocoa solids
300 ml (¹/2 pint) whipping cream

Melt the chocolate in a microwave, following maker's instructions, or in a bowl set over a pan of barely simmering water (the bowl must not touch the water). Using an electric whisk, whip the cream to a soft peaks – not too stiff. Add a third of the whipped cream to the chocolate and whisk to a smooth, even texture. Add the remaining cream, stirring gently with a wooden spoon. Fill the centre of the Saint-Honoré with two-thirds of the cream. Using a piping bag with a smooth 12-mm/¹/2-inch nozzle, decorate the top of the gateau with little swirls of the remaining chocolate cream.

TO SERVE
unsweetened cocoa powder mixed with icing sugar
chocolate shavings

Decorate half the Saint-Honoré with a fine layer of icing sugar mixed with cocoa powder, and sprinkle a few chocolate shavings in the centre.

Profiteroles

Try a new taste sensation with these chocolate profiteroles. The classic recipe for this semi-warm, semi-cold dessert has been slightly varied by adding cocoa powder to the choux pastry. Don't forget to serve a little extra chocolate sauce for any chocoholic guests!

Serves 6

CHOCOLATE CHOUX PASTRY
125 ml (4 fl oz) milk
125 ml (4 fl oz) water
125 g (4$^{1}/_{2}$ oz) unsalted butter, cut into small pieces
$^{1}/_{2}$ teaspoon salt
1 teaspoon caster sugar
165 g (5$^{1}/_{2}$ oz) plain flour
1$^{1}/_{2}$ tablespoons unsweetened cocoa powder
5 eggs
4 tablespoons chopped almonds

Preheat the oven to 190°C (375°F), gas mark 5.
Mix the milk, water, butter, salt and sugar in a pan and bring to the boil. Add the flour and cocoa in one go, stirring in with a wooden spoon for about 2 minutes. Remove from the heat and add the eggs one at a time, stirring each one well in.
Using a piping bag with a 12-mm/$^{1}/_{2}$-inch nozzle, pipe small balls of choux pastry (about the size of a walnut) onto a baking sheet lined with nonstick baking parchment. Sprinkle with chopped almonds and bake in the preheated oven for 20–25 minutes. making sure you do not open the oven door while they are cooking. Remove from the baking sheet and leave to cool on a wire rack.

VANILLA ICE CREAM
500 ml (18 fl oz) milk
200 ml (7 fl oz) whipping cream
175 g (6 oz) caster sugar
2 vanilla pods, split open
7 egg yolks

Put the milk, cream, half the sugar and the vanilla pods into a pan and bring to the boil. Remove from the heat and leave to infuse for 20 minutes.
Beat the egg yolks with the rest of the sugar until the mixture lightens in colour.
Remove the vanilla pods from the infusion and pour the milk onto the egg mixture, whisking continuously. Return the mixture to the pan and heat gently until it thickens and coats the back of a spoon, then pass through a fine-mesh sieve.
Cool in the refrigerator, stirring from time to time, and then churn in an ice-cream maker.

CHOCOLATE SAUCE
125 g (4 oz) best quality dark chocolate,
70% cocoa solids
100 ml (3$^{1}/_{2}$ fl oz) milk
4 tablespoons whipping cream
2 tablespoons caster sugar
$^{1}/_{2}$ tablespoon unsalted butter, cut into small pieces

Chop the chocolate using a knife or food processor and put into a heatproof bowl.
Put the milk, cream and sugar into a pan and bring to the boil. Pour onto the chopped chocolate, whisking briskly. Add the butter and mix carefully to obtain a smooth, shiny texture.

TO ASSEMBLE THE PROFITEROLES
icing sugar

Cut each profiterole in half. Fill the bottom half with a small scoop of vanilla ice cream and cover with the top half. Sprinkle with icing sugar.
Quickly arrange the profiteroles in individual dishes or on a serving dish. Drizzle with hot chocolate sauce and serve immediately.

Twelfth-Night cake

The tradition of Twelfth-Night cake (*Galette des Rois*), eaten in France to celebrate Epiphany, is said to date from Roman times when a festival held on the winter solstice offered everyone an opportunity to be king for a day if their portion of cake contained a lucky charm. The creation of this cake, especially the puff pastry, requires a degree of skill during the *tourage* (rolling and folding process). For the best results, start making the pastry the day before, 'rolling and folding' the mixture four times, and finish the next day, 'rolling and folding' twice. The chocolate version of the cake goes particularly well with raspberries and, accompanied by Champagne, is delicious served warm.

Serves 6

CHOCOLATE PUFF PASTRY

FOR THE DOUGH
30 g (1 oz) unsalted butter
250 g (9 oz) plain flour
1 teaspoon salt
125 ml (4 fl oz) water

FOR THE TOURAGE
250 g (9 oz) unsalted butter
1 1/2 tablespoons icing sugar
3 1/2 tablespoons unsweetened cocoa powder

To make the dough, melt the butter and mix lightly with the flour, salt and water. Blend well and shape into a ball. Cover with clingfilm and chill for 1 hour. Soften the butter for the tourage with a wooden spoon, then add the icing sugar and cocoa. Shape into a block, cover with clingfilm and chill for 1 hour. Remove from the refrigerator before the next stage so that it will spread easily. Now, the tourage process begins. Flour the work surface and roll out the dough into a 20-cm/ 8-inch square. Spread the tourage butter over half the sheet, fold over the second half to enclose the butter, and roll the dough into a rectangle, 50 cm/20 inches by 20 cm/8 inches. Fold into three, folding one end into the centre and the other end over that. Give the pastry a quarter turn and, with the rolling pin at right angles to the folds, repeat the 'roll and fold' process twice more. Chill for 1 hour. Repeat the 'roll and fold' sequence twice more, ensuring the pastry is chilled in the refrigerator for at least 1 hour between each sequence. Altogether, the pastry should be 'rolled and folded' 6 times.

GLAZE
(Makes 50 ml/2 fl oz)
2 egg yolks
1 tablespoon milk
pinch of salt

Whisk all the ingredients together with an electric whisk.

CHOCOLATE FRANGIPANE
85 g (3 oz) unsalted butter
85 g (3 oz) ground almonds
85 g (3 oz) caster sugar
1 egg, beaten
2 tablespoons cornflour
100 g (3 1/2 oz) confectioners' custard (see recipe p. 20)
2 tablespoons dark rum
85 g (3 oz) best quality dark chocolate, 70% cocoa solids

Cream the butter. Add the ground almonds, sugar and beaten egg, and mix well. Then stir in the cornflour, confectioners' custard and rum. Melt the chocolate in a microwave, following the maker's instructions, or in a bowl set over a pan of barely simmering water (the bowl must not touch the water). Add to the frangipane and mix well.

TO ASSEMBLE AND BAKE THE CAKE
3 tablespoons raspberry jam with seeds
1 lucky charm, wrapped in baking parchment
2 tablespoons glaze (take from recipe on this page)

Divide the pastry in two and roll each half to a thickness of 2 mm/1/16 inch. Cut two rounds, each 26 cm/10 1/2 inches in diameter, and place one on a baking sheet lined with nonstick baking parchment. Spread evenly with the frangipane, leaving a 2-cm/ 3/4-inch border around the edge. Top with a layer of raspberry jam and insert the charm (always warn unsuspecting guests!). Brush the pastry border with glaze and place the second round on top of the first, making sure you give it a quarter turn. Then press the edges firmly together so that they are well sealed. Glaze the top of the cake and crimp the edges. Chill in the refrigerator for 1 hour.
Preheat the oven to 190°C (375°F), gas mark 5.
Glaze the top once more and then, using a small knife, draw a pattern of curved lines from the centre to the edges. Bake in the preheated oven at 40–45 minutes. Leave to cool on a wire rack.

Chocolate macaroons

These little cakes, crunchy on the outside and deliciously soft on the inside, have existed for hundreds of years. The recipe originated in Italy, especially Venice, during the Renaissance (the name derives from the Italian *maccherone* and the Venetian *macarone*, meaning 'fine paste'). The chocolate ganache, which can be replaced by a number of other fillings, for example chocolate banana jam or raspberry jam, is really easy to make. However, the same cannot be said for the macaroons, and mixing the ingredients is a particularly delicate operation.

Makes 50 small macaroons

MACAROONS
230 g (8 oz) ground almonds
320 g (11½ oz) icing sugar
5 tablespoons unsweetened cocoa powder
7 egg whites
150 g (5 oz) caster sugar

Process the ground almonds, icing sugar and cocoa in an electric blender to obtain an extremely fine powder. Using an electric whisk, beat the egg whites and sugar until they form stiff peaks. Carefully incorporate the cocoa mixture with a wooden spoon, mixing downwards to the centre of the bowl, then up to the edges and back toward the centre, until you obtain a smooth, even texture.
Using a piping bag, pipe small, evenly sized balls of the macaroon mixture onto a baking sheet lined with nonstick baking parchment. Leave to stand at room temperature for 30 minutes.
Preheat the oven to 180°C (350°F), gas mark 4 and bake the macaroons for 10–13 minutes. Remove from the baking sheet and leave to cool on a wire rack.

CHOCOLATE GANACHE
325 g (12 oz) best quality dark chocolate, 70% cocoa solids
230 ml (8 fl oz) double cream

Chop the chocolate using a knife or food processor and place in a heatproof bowl.
Pour the cream into a pan, bring to the boil and pour onto the chopped chocolate. Mix well to obtain a smooth, shiny texture. Leave to cool at room temperature so that the ganache remains workable.

TO ASSEMBLE THE MACAROONS
Stick the macaroons together in pairs with chocolate ganache and chill in the refrigerator.

Kouglofs

It would be impossible to mention the regional specialities of Alsace without including these variedly spelled (kougelhopf, gougelhopf, kugelhopf) yeast cakes made with raisins and traditionally eaten at Sunday breakfast, although Germany, Austria and Poland also claim credit for them. There are special moulds for these cakes but if you can find terracotta ones, they give a more evenly distributed heat and a more authentic flavour.

Makes 2 x 450 g (1 lb) cakes

55 g (2 oz) raisins
1 tablespoon dark rum
275 g (9³/4 oz) plain flour
3 1/2 tablespoons unsweetened cocoa powder
170 g (6 oz) caster sugar
pinch of salt
20 g (³/4 oz) fresh yeast (if using equivalent dried yeast, follow the maker's instructions)
1 egg + 1 egg yolk
140 ml (4¹/2 fl oz) milk
240 g (8¹/2 oz) unsalted butter, cut into small pieces
50 g (1³/4 oz) chocolate chips
40 g (1¹/2 oz) almonds, chopped
25 g (1 oz) ground cinnamon

Soak the raisins in the rum.

Heat the milk to blood heat and pour into the bowl of an electric mixer, crumble in the fresh yeast and stir until it is dissolved. (If using dried yeast, follow the maker's instructions.) Add the flour, cocoa, 2 tablespoons of sugar, salt, egg and egg yolk. Using the dough hook, starting at low speed and gradually building up to moderate, knead for about 10 minutes or until the mixture is elastic and smooth, (Alternatively, mix well in a bowl and knead by hand.)

When the dough begins to come away from the sides of the bowl, add 140 g (5 oz) of the butter, piece by piece. Continue to knead slowly until the butter is thoroughly worked into the dough. Then add the soaked raisins and chocolate chips, and leave the dough to rise at room temperature for 1 hour.

Butter two 18-cm/7-inch kouglof moulds or deep ring moulds, and sprinkle the insides with the chopped almonds.

Knead the air out of the dough and divide in two. On a floured work surface roll and form one of the pieces of dough into a sausage shape with floured hands and place gently in the base of the mould. Repeat the process with the other half of the dough and place in the second mould.

Set aside and leave to rise for 1¹/2–2 hours at room temperature – the dough should rise almost to the top of the moulds.

Preheat the oven to 190°C (375°F), gas mark 5. Bake the kouglofs in the preheated oven for 40–45 minutes. Remove from the oven, turn the cakes out of the moulds and leave to cool on a wire rack.

Melt the remaining butter and use to brush the kouglofs. Sprinkle with the remaining sugar mixed with the ground cinnamon.

Concorde

This delicious dessert consists of alternate layers of meringue and chocolate mousse. The simultaneously crunchy and soft texture of the meringue combines with the frothiness of the chocolate mousse filling to create an extremely pleasant sensation in the mouth. The meringue, which you may prefer 'plain' (flavoured with vanilla sugar), can be prepared in advance, provided it is kept dry in an airtight container.

Serves 6

CHOCOLATE MERINGUE

4 egg whites
125 g (4 oz) caster sugar
100 g (3½ oz) icing sugar
3½ tablespoons unsweetened cocoa powder

Using an electric whisk, beat the egg whites until they form stiff peaks, adding the caster sugar about half way through.
Sift the icing sugar and cocoa together and stir gently into the egg whites.
Preheated the oven to 140°C (275°F), gas mark 1.
Using a piping bag with a 12-mm/½-inch nozzle, pipe two discs of meringue, 16 cm/6 inches in diameter, onto a baking sheet lined with nonstick baking parchment. Change to a 4-mm/⅛-inch nozzle and pipe the rest of the meringue into thin sausage shapes, making sure they are spaced well apart.
Bake in the preheated oven for 1½ hours. The meringue should be dry and brittle. Remove from the baking sheet and leave to cool on a wire rack.

CRÈME ANGLAISE CUSTARD

2 egg yolks
2 tablespoons caster sugar
90 ml (3½ fl oz) milk
90 ml (3½ fl oz) whipping cream

Beat the egg yolks and sugar in a heatproof bowl until the mixture lightens in colour. Pour the milk and cream into a pan, bring to the boil and pour onto the beaten egg mixture, whisking continuously. Return the mixture to the pan and heat gently until it thickens and coats the back of a spoon. Pass through a fine-mesh sieve and leave to cool.

CHOCOLATE MOUSSE

200 g (7 oz) best quality dark chocolate,
70% cocoa solids
200 ml (7 fl oz) crème anglaise custard (see recipe left)
300 ml (½ pint) whipping cream

Chop the chocolate using a knife or food processor and put into a heatproof bowl. Heat the crème anglaise custard and pour onto the chocolate, mixing well. Using an electric whisk beat the cream to a soft consistency – it should be frothy and not too stiff. Whisk a third of the whipped cream into the warm chocolate and custard mixture (40–45°C/104–113°F), then stir in the rest of the cream.

TO ASSEMBLE THE CONCORDE

unsweetened cocoa powder

Place one of the meringue discs in a flan ring, 18 cm/ 7 inches in diameter and 4 cm/1½ inches deep. Cover with a layer of chocolate mousse to half the depth of the ring, then add the second meringue disc and another layer of mousse – this layer should be level with the top of the flan ring.
Chill in the refrigerator for 4 hours.
To serve, remove the ring, cut the meringue 'sausages' into sticks about 2 cm/¾ inch long and use them to cover the surface and sides of the gateau. Dust with cocoa powder.

Mille-feuille

In this dessert, the chocolate subtly underscores the smoothness of the confectioners' custard and the lightness of the puff pastry. To ensure the pastry remains crisp, don't add the filling until the last minute. Adding the confectioners' custard too early would totally ruin the crisp, light texture of the mille-feuille. See the recipe for Twelfth-Night Cake on p. 62 for an explanation of the tourage 'roll and fold' process.

Serves 6

CHOCOLATE PUFF PASTRY

FOR THE DOUGH
30 g (1 oz) unsalted butter
250 g (9 oz) plain flour
1 teaspoon salt
125 ml (4 fl oz) water

FOR THE TOURAGE
250 g (9 oz) unsalted butter
$1^1/2$ tablespoons icing sugar
$3^1/2$ tablespoons unsweetened cocoa powder

To make the dough, melt the butter and mix lightly with the flour, salt and water. When all the ingredients are well blended, shape the dough into a ball, cover with clingfilm and chill in the refrigerator for 1 hour. Soften the butter for the tourage with a wooden spoon, then adding the icing sugar and cocoa. Shape into a block, cover with clingfilm and chill in the refrigerator for 1 hour. Remove from the refrigerator before the next stage to allow it to become spreadable.
Now, the tourage process begins. Flour the work surface and roll out the dough into a 20 cm/8 inch square. Spread the tourage butter over half the sheet, fold over the second half to enclose the butter, and roll the dough into a rectangle, 50 cm/20 inches long by 20 cm/ 8 inches wide. Fold into three by folding one end into the centre and then the other end over that. Give the pastry a quarter turn and, with the rolling pin at right angles to the folds, repeat the 'roll and fold' process twice more. Chill in the refrigerator for 1 hour.
Repeat the tourage 'roll and fold' sequences twice more, making sure you chill the pastry in the refrigerator for at least 1 hour between each set of sequences. Altogether, the pastry should be 'rolled and folded' 6 times.
Roll the pastry to a thickness of 2 mm/$1/16$ inch and cut into three 22-cm/$8^1/2$-inch squares. Place on a baking sheet lined with nonstick baking parchment and prick all over with a fork. Chill in the refrigerator for 1 hour.
Preheat the oven to 200°C (400°F), gas mark 6 and bake the pastry squares for about 20 minutes. Remove from the baking sheet and leave to cool on a wire rack.

CHOCOLATE CONFECTIONERS' CUSTARD

120 g ($4^1/2$ oz) best quality dark chocolate, 70% cocoa solids
600 g (1 lb 5 oz) confectioners' custard (see recipe p. 20)
4 tablespoons whipping cream

Melt the chocolate in a microwave, following the maker's instructions, or in a bowl set over a pan of barely simmering water (the bowl must not touch the water). Warm the confectioners' custard and add the chocolate to the custard. Then add the whipping cream, mixing well to obtain a smooth, creamy texture.

TO ASSEMBLE THE MILLE-FEUILLE

icing sugar
unsweetened cocoa powder
dark chocolate shavings

Trim the three layers of puff pastry so that each is 20 cm/8 inches square.
Using a piping bag with a smooth 12-mm/$1/2$-inch nozzle, pipe half the confectioners' custard onto the first layer. Cover with a second layer of mille-feuille and pipe on the rest of the confectioners' custard. Top with the third layer of pastry, placing the smoothest side uppermost.
Decorate the top of the mille-feuille by dividing it diagonally, and dusting one half with icing sugar and the other with cocoa powder. Scatter a few chocolate shavings in the centre. Dividing into portions will be easier using a serrated knife.

Envy

It's Christmas morning and everyone is gathered around the tree, impatient to open their presents. Grandma is waiting for hers, eyes shining expectantly. The children run from parcel to parcel, exclaiming excitedly. Grandma laughs indulgently and starts to open her presents with an air of feigned detachment. Suddenly, she stops and stares, her face transfixed, distorted by envy. Her neighbour on the sofa has just unwrapped a huge box of chocolates – one of those boxes containing layers of sheer self-indulgence that she adores. 'Grandma, we thought Great Aunt Alice could have the chocolates this year, just for a change. You're not disappointed, are you?'

'Envy is one of the classic deadly sins that prevents us from truly rejoicing in the good fortune of others.' (La Rochefoucauld)

Madeleines

The origin of these small tea cakes is the subject of much debate. According to one theory, they were created – and named after – a young peasant girl in the French region of Lorraine, where they came to the notice of Duke Stanislas Leszczynski and were introduced to the French court by his daughter, who was married to Louis XV. Today, baking madeleines is much easier since the modern silicon versions of the ribbed oval moulds that given them their rounded, shell-like appearance do not need to be buttered or floured. Madeleines were immortalized by the French writer, Marcel Proust, who described how a piece of this 'seashell cake so strictly pleated on the outside and so sensual inside' eaten with a spoonful of tea caused childhood memories to come flooding back. (*Remembrance of Things Past*)

Makes approximately 35 madeleines

250 g (9 oz) unsalted butter
30 g (1 oz) best quality dark chocolate,
70% cocoa solids
3 eggs
160 g (5$^1/_2$ oz) caster sugar
1$^1/_2$ tablespoons clear honey
5 tablespoons milk
225 g (8 oz) plain flour
2 teaspoons baking powder
3$^1/_2$ tablespoons unsweetened cocoa powder

Prepare the madeleine mixture 24 hours in advance. Heat the butter in a pan until it turns a light nut-brown colour.
Melt the chocolate in a microwave, following the maker's instructions, or in a bowl set over a pan of barely simmering water (the bowl must not touch the water).
Using a balloon whisk, beat the eggs, sugar, honey and milk together in a mixing bowl. Add the sifted flour, cocoa and baking powder, and mix well. Then stir in the warm butter and melted chocolate.
Chill in the refrigerator overnight.
The next day, preheat the oven to 220°C (425°F), gas mark 7. Lightly butter and flour the madeleine moulds (unless they are silicon moulds) and, using a spoon, two-thirds fill each mould with the mixture.
Cook in the preheated oven for 10–12 minutes. Remove from the moulds and leave to cool on a wire rack.

Temptation

An elegant and sophisticated creation that will do justice to any dinner party. Although it requires a certain degree of skill, it is possible to simplify things at the icing stage. Instead of icing the cake – always a fairly delicate operation – you can simply dust it with unsweetened cocoa powder and decorate with chopped pistachio nuts. This is a dessert for those extra special occasions – the chocolate-brownie sponge is covered with pistachio cream and then the whole cake coated with a layer of chocolate mousse.

Serves 6

CHOCOLATE-BROWNIE SPONGE
35 g (1¼ oz) best quality dark chocolate, 70% cocoa solids
60 g (2¼ oz) unsalted butter, creamed
1 egg
30 g (1 oz) caster sugar
30 g (1 oz) soft dark brown sugar
30 g (1 oz) plain flour
40 g (1½ oz) chopped walnuts

Preheat the oven to 180°C (350°F), gas mark 4.
Melt the chocolate in a microwave, following the maker's instructions, or in a bowl set over a pan of barely simmering water (the bowl must not touch the water).
Add the butter and mix well to a smooth consistency. Then incorporate the egg, caster sugar and soft brown sugar. Add the flour and chopped walnuts, mixing well to obtain a smooth, even texture.
Turn the mixture into a 16-cm/6-inch flan ring on a baking sheet lined with nonstick baking parchment. Cook in the preheated oven for about 15 minutes – the sponge should remain springy to the touch – and then leave to cool in the flan ring.

PISTACHIO CREAM
1 gelatine leaf (powdered gelatine: use ¼ of an 11-g sachet and follow maker's instructions for dissolving)
2 egg yolks
1½ tablespoons caster sugar
3 tablespoons double cream
15 g (½ oz) pistachio paste

Soften the gelatine leaf by soaking in cold water. (If using powdered gelatine, follow the maker's instructions for dissolving.)
Beat the egg yolks and caster sugar in a heatproof bowl until the mixture lightens in colour.
Bring the cream to the boil and pour onto the egg mixture. Return the mixture to the pan and stir over low heat until it thickens and coats the back of a spoon. Squeeze the excess water from the gelatine and add to the pan with the pistachio paste. (If using powdered gelatine, add the dissolved powder to the pan.)
Stir to dissolve.

Process the mixture in an electric blender and chill in the refrigerator.
When the cream begins to set, smooth it over the brownie sponge with a palette knife. Then put the whole cake (still in the ring) into the freezer.

CHOCOLATE MOUSSE
110 g (3¾ oz) best quality dark chocolate, 70% cocoa solids
3 egg yolks
50 ml (2 fl oz) syrup (see recipe p. 30)
200 ml (7 fl oz) double cream

Melt the chocolate in a microwave, following the maker's instructions, or in a bowl set over a pan of barely simmering water (the bowl must not touch the water).
Put the egg yolks into a heatproof bowl, bring the syrup to the boil and pour gradually onto the egg yolks, whisking briskly with a balloon whisk or an electric whisk until the mixture doubles in volume.
Using a clean whisk, whip the cream – it should be light and frothy and not too stiff.
Whisk a third of the whipped cream into the warm, melted chocolate. Then, using a wooden spoon, incorporate the egg-and-syrup mixture, and the rest of the cream.
Remove the cake from the ring and place on a baking sheet. Cover the top and sides of the cake with the mousse and leave to set in the freezer.

TO ASSEMBLE THE CAKE
400 g (14 oz) chocolate icing (see recipe p. 40)
10 small chocolate macaroons
10 g (¼ oz) pistachios, chopped

Take the cake out of the freezer, slide it off the baking sheet and place on a wire rack, putting the baking sheet under the rack to catch any drips.
Cover the cake with warm icing (30–35°C/86–95°F), smoothing the top and sides with a palette knife. Decorate with halved macaroons and sprinkle with chopped pistachios. Leave to defrost completely in the refrigerator for 8 hours before serving.

Chocolate and salted-caramel tart

A surprisingly sucessful combination of sweet shortcrust pastry filled with salted-caramel cream, dark chocolate Chantilly and hazelnut crunch. The crunchy sea salt and hazelnuts, the frothy Chantilly and the smooth caramel cream offer a contrast of textures and flavours that will delight your palate. It's important to make a dark caramel (170–180°C/ 338–356°F), as it has a much richer flavour. If you prefer, you can make individual tartlets.

Serves 6

SWEET SHORTCRUST PASTRY

150 g (5 oz) unsalted butter
250 g (9 oz) plain flour
30 g (1 oz) ground almonds
90 g (3¼ oz) icing sugar
1 egg, beaten
pinch of salt

Rub the butter into the flour with your fingertips to a light, crumbly mixture. Add the ground almonds and sugar, then the egg and salt, and mix lightly to a smooth, even dough. Chill for several hours (12 hours if you can). Preheat the oven to 180°C (350°F), gas mark 4. Roll out the pastry to a thickness of 3 mm/⅛ inch and use to line a flan dish, 22 cm/8½ inches in diameter by 2 cm/¾ inch deep. Prick the base with a fork. Bake for 20–25 minutes then remove and leave to cool.

HAZELNUT CRUNCH

200 g (7 oz) preserving sugar (with added pectin)
3½ tablespoons water
100 g (3½ oz) unsalted butter
100 g (3½ oz) chopped hazelnuts
pinch of sea salt

Preheat the oven to 160°C (325°F), gas mark 3. Put the sugar, water and butter in a pan and bring to the boil. Spread a 2–3 mm/1/16–⅛ inch layer of the mixture on a baking sheet lined with nonstick baking parchment. Sprinkle with the hazelnuts and sea salt. Bake in the preheated oven for about 15 minutes, until it turns a caramel colour. Remove from the oven and leave to cool.

SALTED-CARAMEL CREAM

2 gelatine leaves (powdered gelatine: use half an 11-g sachet and follow maker's instructions for dissolving)
250 ml (9 fl oz) whipping cream
100 g (3½ oz) caster sugar
4 egg yolks
60 g (2¼ oz) slightly salted butter, cut into small pieces
pinch of sea salt

Soften the gelatine leaf by soaking in cold water. (If using powdered gelatine, follow the maker's instructions for dissolving.) Bring the cream to the boil. Put the sugar in a separate pan without any liquid and bring to the boil, stirring continuously with a wooden spoon to obtain a caramel, then add the hot cream to lower the cooking temperature and give the caramel the required consistency.
Put the egg yolks in a heatproof bowl and add the caramel mixture, beating briskly with a balloon whisk. Return the mixture to the pan and stir over low heat until it thickens and coats the back of a spoon. Squeeze the excess water from the gelatine and add to the pan with the butter and sea salt. (If using powdered gelatine, add the dissolved powder to the pan.) Process in an electric blender and leave to cool. When the cream begins to set, turn into the cooked tart base, spread evenly with a palette knife and chill in the refrigerator.

DARK CHOCOLATE CHANTILLY CREAM

100 g (3½ oz) best quality dark chocolate, 70% cocoa solids
200 ml (7 fl oz) whipping cream

Melt the chocolate in a microwave, following the maker's instructions, or in a bowl set over a pan of barely simmering water (the bowl must not touch the water). Whip the cream using an electric whisk – it should be light and frothy and not too stiff. Add a third of the whipped cream to the melted chocolate and whisk until you obtain a smooth even texture. Then carefully incorporate the rest of the cream using a wooden spoon.
Using a piping bag with a smooth 12-mm/½-inch nozzle, cover the surface of the tart with Chantilly cream rosettes.

TO SERVE

Break the hazelnut crunch into 3–4 cm/1¼–1½-inch pieces and dot about the surface of the tart at irregular intervals.

White-chocolate 'brownies' with raspberries

In this original interpretation of the traditional chocolate-brownie recipe, the sweetness of the white chocolate and fresh fruit flavour of the raspberries cannot fail to delight anyone who likes unusual cakes and desserts or who simply likes to try something a little different.

Makes 20 'brownies'

170 g (6 oz) white chocolate
315 g (11 oz) unsalted butter, creamed
5 eggs
400 g (14 oz) caster sugar
225 g (8 oz) plain flour
175 g (6 oz) chopped unblanched almonds
100 g (3¹/₂ oz) raspberries
2 tablespoons icing sugar

Preheat the oven to 180°C (350°F), gas mark 4.
Melt the chocolate in a microwave, following the maker's instructions, or in a bowl set over a pan of barely simmering water (the bowl must not touch the water). Add the butter and mix well to obtain a smooth texture. Incorporate the eggs and caster sugar, then the flour and chopped almonds. Mix well to obtain an evenly textured mixture.
Butter the sides of a rectangular baking tin – 36 cm/ 14¹/₄ inches long by 26 cm/10¹/₂ inches wide and 2.5 cm/1 inch deep – and line the base with nonstick baking parchment.
Pour in the cake mixture and sprinkle with raspberries. Bake in the preheated oven for 20–22 minutes and then leave to cool in the tin. Cut into portions and decorate with a light dusting of icing sugar.
You can vary the shape of the 'brownies' by using differently shaped bun tins.

Truffles

Although truffles tend to be enjoyed with an after-dinner cup of coffee and are traditionally given at Christmas, it has to be said that intense 'chocolate moments' can be experienced at any hour of the day or time of year. You can flavour the truffles by infusing the cream with cinnamon (3 sticks), Earl Grey tea (2–3 teabags), or vanilla (2 pods).

Makes 40 truffles

340 g (11¾ oz) best quality dark chocolate, 70% cocoa solids
80 g (2¾ oz) best quality unsweetened cocoa powder
200 ml (7 fl oz) double cream
35 g (1¼ oz) unsalted butter, cut into small pieces

Melt the chocolate in a microwave, following the maker's instructions, or in a bowl set over a pan of barely simmering water (the bowl must not touch the water). Set aside and keep warm.

Bring the cream to the boil and pour onto the chocolate whisking briskly with a balloon whisk. Add the butter and whisk again.

Pour the mixture into a dish lined with nonstick baking parchment, to a depth of 2 cm/¾ inch. Chill in the refrigerator overnight.

The next day, remove the truffle mixture from the dish and cut into 2-cm/¾-inch squares. Roll into balls and coat with cocoa powder. Some can be rolled in icing sugar for a contrast, if desired.

Chill in the refrigerator.

Chocolate mousse

This dessert certainly has a number of points in its favour. Not only is it easy to make, it can also be prepared the day before. Most people like it and it makes a light finish to any meal. This classic version can easily be given extra flavour by adding orange rind or pieces of candied orange peel. You can also flavour the cream by infusing it with spices (see introduction to Truffles, p. 82).

Serves 6

250 g (9 oz) best quality dark chocolate,
70% cocoa solids
100 ml (3½ fl oz) whipping cream
6 egg whites
3 tablespoons caster sugar

Peel off a few chocolate shavings with a vegetable peeler and set aside for decoration. Melt the chocolate in a microwave, following the maker's instructions, or in a bowl set over a pan of barely simmering water (the bowl must not touch the water).
Bring the whipping cream to the boil and pour onto the melted chocolate, beating briskly with a balloon whisk.
Beat the egg whites with the caster sugar until they form stiff peaks.
Add a quarter of the egg whites to the chocolate mixture, whisking well in. Then gently fold in the remaining egg whites to achieve a smooth, even texture.
Turn into a serving dish or individual glass dishes and chill in the refrigerator for 3 hours.
Just before serving, decorate with chocolate shavings

Paris-Brest

In 1891, a Parisian pastrycook had the idea of naming his latest creation after the bicycle race between Paris and Brest. This ring-shaped cake, reminiscent of a bicycle wheel, is traditionally made from choux pastry, filled with praline-flavoured cream and sprinkled with flaked almonds. This version, filled with chocolate butter cream, works just as well, especially when served warm.

Serves 6

CHOUX PASTRY

125 ml (4 fl oz) milk
125 ml (4 fl oz) water
125 g (4$^1/_2$ oz) unsalted butter, cut into small pieces
pinch of salt
1 teaspoon caster sugar
165 g (5$^1/_2$ oz) plain flour
5 eggs
1 egg yolk mixed with 1 tablespoon milk
50 g (2 oz) flaked almonds – baked on a sheet at 200°C/400°F/gas mark 6 until golden
20 g ($^3/_4$ oz) sugar nibs or candy sugar

Preheat the oven to 190°C (375°F), gas mark 5.
Mix the milk, water, butter, salt and caster sugar together in a pan and bring to the boil. Add the flour in one go and beat in with a wooden spoon for about 2 minutes. Remove from the heat. Add the whole eggs one at a time, stirring each one well in.
Using a piping bag with a 14-mm/$^5/_8$-inch nozzle, pipe a ring of pastry, 18 cm/7 inches in diameter, onto a baking sheet lined with nonstick baking parchment. Pipe a second ring immediately inside the first. Pipe a third ring on top of the other two, along the line of the join. Brush over the rings with the egg and milk glaze. Sprinkle with the toasted almonds and sugar nibs.
Cook in the preheated oven for 25–30 minutes, making sure you do not open the oven door during cooking. Remove from the oven and leave to cool.

CHOCOLATE BUTTER CREAM

50 g (2 oz) best quality dark chocolate, 70% cocoa solids
250 g (9 oz) confectioners' custard (see recipe p. 20)
150 g (5 oz) unsalted butter

Melt the chocolate in a microwave, following the maker's instructions, or in a bowl set over a pan of barely simmering water (the bowl must not touch the water). Warm the confectioners' custard and add the melted chocolate to the custard.
Cream the butter in an electric blender, or food processor using the whisk attachment. Then add the chocolate confectioners' custard, and whisk to obtain a smooth, even texture.

TO ASSEMBLE THE PARIS-BREST
icing sugar

Cut the choux-pastry ring in half horizontally using a serrated knife.
Using a piping bag with a 12-mm/$^1/_2$-inch fluted nozzle, pipe swirls of chocolate butter cream onto the inner and outer rings of the base.
Replace the top, pressing down gently to make a good contact but not so that the filling oozes out, and dust with icing sugar.

Avarice

A few Smarties carefully concealed in a child's handkerchief at playtime, a bar of chocolate kept in its wrapper and nibbled when alone, chocolate liqueurs to be savoured in secret to avoid envious looks and scroungers – this is when indulgence becomes avarice. And what better example of avarice than Harpagon – the miser created by the 17th-century French playwright, Molière – who fills his cash box with gold (or maybe they were chocolate) coins but is reluctant to fill his guests' dinner plates:

'Maître Jacques: How many will there be for dinner?

Harpagon: Eight or ten, but only provide food for eight.

When there's enough food for eight, there's plenty enough for ten.'

(*The Miser*, Molière)

Chocolate goblets

With its contrasting textures and temperatures, this dessert combines chocolate in a number of different guises. Chocolate lovers will be unable to resist its subtle variations. The goblets are lined with chocolate ganache sprinkled with chocolate crumble. Then come the melting texture of the chocolate sorbet and a delicate coating of chocolate sauce interspersed with pieces of chocolate crumble (you don't need to dip the goblets in chocolate as shown in the picture opposite, except for decorative purposes of course!).

Makes 6 goblets

CREAMY CHOCOLATE GANACHE
140 g (5 oz) best quality dark chocolate,
70% cocoa solids
200 ml (7 fl oz) double cream
200 ml (7 fl oz) milk
5 egg yolks
3 tablespoons caster sugar

Chop the chocolate in using a knife or food processor and place in a heatproof bowl. Mix the cream and milk in a pan and bring to the boil.
Place the egg yolks and sugar in a heatproof basin and beat until the mixture lightens in colour, then whisk in the boiling milk and cream. Return the mixture to the pan and stir over low heat until it thickens and coats the back of a spoon. Pour onto the chopped chocolate and mix until all the chocolate has melted, then process in an electric blender or food processor for a few seconds.
Divide the ganache between 6 glass goblets taking care not to get any on the outsides or rims.
Chill in the refrigerator for 3 hours.

CHOCOLATE CRUMBLE
15 g (1/2 oz) dark chocolate chips
70 g (21/2 oz) plain flour
1 tablespoon unsweetened cocoa powder
50 g (2 oz) unsalted butter
3 tablespoons soft brown sugar
pinch of salt
pinch of ground cinnamon

Preheat the oven to 180°C (350°F), gas mark 4.
Put all the ingredients in a mixing bowl and rub lightly with your fingertips until you have a coarse, crumbly mixture. Chill in the refrigerator for 1 hour.
Spread the crumble evenly on a baking sheet lined with nonstick baking parchment.
Cook in the preheated oven for 15–20 minutes. Remove from the oven and leave to cool.

CHOCOLATE SORBET
120 g (41/4 oz) best quality dark chocolate,
70% cocoa solids
6 tablespoons unsweetened cocoa powder
125 g (4 oz) caster sugar
300 ml (1/2 pint) water

Chop the chocolate using a knife or food processor and place in a heatproof bowl with the cocoa powder. Put the sugar and water in a pan and bring to the boil. Pour the syrup onto the chocolate and cocoa, whisking briskly with a balloon whisk.
Churn the mixture in an ice-cream maker and chill in the refrigerator.

CHOCOLATE SAUCE
60 g (21/4 oz) best quality dark chocolate,
70% cocoa solids
31/2 tablespoons milk
11/2 tablespoons whipping cream
1 tablespoon caster sugar
1 teaspoon unsalted butter

Chop the chocolate using a knife or food processor and put in a heatproof bowl. Put the milk, cream and sugar in pan and bring to the boil. Pour the mixture onto the chopped chocolate, whisking briskly with a balloon whisk. Add the butter and mix well in to obtain a smooth, shiny sauce.

TO ASSEMBLE THE GOBLETS
chocolate shavings

Lightly crush the crumble and sprinkle a few pieces on the ganache in the goblets. Add a scoop of chocolate sorbet and then cover with a coating of warm chocolate sauce.
To finish, sprinkle with a few chocolate shavings and pieces of crumble. Serve immediately.

Liégeois

'Café liégeois' is a classic iced coffee dessert that successfully combines indulgence and elegance. In this chocolate version, the chilled chocolate and chocolate ice cream offer a delicious contrast to the warm chocolate sauce and gently melting texture of the vanilla-flavoured Chantilly cream. A dessert that will appeal to chocoholics of all ages.

Serves 6

DARK CHOCOLATE ICE CREAM
150 g (5 oz) best quality dark chocolate,
70% cocoa solids
500 ml (18 fl oz) milk
100 ml (3½ fl oz) whipping cream
150 g (5 oz) caster sugar
5 egg yolks

Chop the chocolate using a knife or food processor and put in a heatproof bowl.
Put the milk, cream and half the sugar into a pan and bring to the boil. Beat the egg yolks with the rest of the sugar in a heatproof bowl until the mixture lightens in colour, then whisk in the boiling milk. Return the mixture to the pan and stir over low heat until it thickens and coats the back of a spoon, then pour onto the chopped chocolate and mix until the chocolate has completely melted.
Leave to cool in the refrigerator, stirring from time to time, and then churn in an ice-cream maker.

CHILLED CHOCOLATE
80 g (2¾ oz) best quality dark chocolate,
70% cocoa solids
250 ml (9 fl oz) milk
60 ml (2¼ fl oz) whipping cream
1 tablespoon soft light brown sugar

Chop the chocolate finely using a knife or food processor and put in a heatproof bowl. Put the milk and cream in a pan and bring to the boil. Pour the mixture carefully onto the chopped chocolate, whisking briskly with a balloon whisk.
Stir in the sugar and leave to cool.

DARK CHOCOLATE SAUCE
60 g (2¼ oz) best quality dark chocolate,
70% cocoa solids
3½ tablespoons milk
1½ tablespoons whipping cream
1 tablespoon caster sugar
1 teaspoon unsalted butter

Chop the chocolate using a knife or food processor and put in a heatproof bowl. Put the milk, cream and sugar in a pan and bring to the boil. Pour onto the chopped chocolate, whisking briskly with a balloon whisk. Add the butter and mix well to obtain a smooth, shiny sauce.

VANILLA-FLAVOURED CHANTILLY CREAM
1 vanilla pod
300 ml (½ pint) whipping cream
25 g (1 oz) icing sugar

Split open the vanilla pod and scrape out the seeds with the point of a knife. Put the cream, icing sugar and vanilla seeds in a mixing bowl and whisk with an electric whisk until it has a light, creamy consistency.

TO ASSEMBLE THE LIÉGEOIS
unsweetened cocoa powder

Divide the cold chocolate between 6 tall glasses and then add two scoops of chocolate ice cream to each glass. Cover with warm chocolate sauce and top with Chantilly cream. Decorate with a dusting of cocoa powder. Serve immediately.

Chocolate and poached-pear tart

Served warm, this dessert – which successfully combines the complementary flavours of the wine, spices, chocolate and fruit – will delight the most discerning palates.
A light, red Beaujolais (Brouilly for example or, in season, a Beaujolais Nouveau) makes an ideal accompaniment.

Serves 6

SWEET SHORTCRUST PASTRY
150 g (5 oz) unsalted butter
250 g (9 oz) plain flour
30 g (1 oz) ground almonds
90 g (3¼ oz) icing sugar
1 egg, beaten
pinch of salt

Rub the butter into the flour with your fingertips until you have a light, crumbly mixture. Add the ground almonds and icing sugar, then the egg and salt, and mix lightly to obtain a smooth, evenly textured dough. Chill in the refrigerator for several hours (12 hours if possible).
Preheat the oven to 180°C (350°F), gas mark 4.
Roll out the pastry to a thickness of 3 mm/⅛ inch and use to line a flan dish, 22 cm/8½ inches in diameter and 2 cm/¾ inch deep. Prick the pastry base with a fork. Bake in the preheated oven for 20–25 minutes then remove and leave to cool.

CHOCOLATE GANACHE WITH RED WINE
140 g (5 oz) best quality dark chocolate, 70% cocoa solids
125 ml (4 fl oz) double cream
50 g (1¾ oz) unsalted butter, cut into small pieces
3 tablespoons light, red Beaujolais

Chop the chocolate using a knife or food processor and put in a heatproof bowl.
Bring the cream to the boil, pour onto the chopped chocolate and mix until the chocolate has completely melted. Carefully mix in the butter, a piece at a time, and then incorporate the wine to obtain a smooth, even texture.
Pour the ganache into the precooked tart case and chill in the refrigerator for 30 minutes.

PEARS POACHED IN WINE
3 pears
400 ml (14 fl oz) light, red Beaujolais
175 g (6 oz) caster sugar
1 cinnamon stick
1 vanilla pod, split open
1 star anise

Peel and halve the pears and remove the core.
Put the wine, sugar, cinnamon, vanilla, and star anise in a pan and bring to the boil.
Add the pears to the syrup and cook over low heat for 15–20 minutes, taking care not to overcook them – they should remain slightly firm. Leave to macerate overnight in the refrigerator.

TO FINISH
icing sugar
chocolate shavings

Drain and then thinly slice the pears.
Arrange in concentric circles on the surface of the tart. Dust the edges of the tart with icing sugar and decorate with chocolate shavings in the centre.

If you prefer, you can make 6 individual tartlets rather than one large tart.

Red-fruit chocolate muffins

Muffins make an ideal accompaniment for afternoon tea or a coffee break. They are quick and easy to make and can be served cold or slightly warm, depending on your taste. In this recipe they are made with chocolate chips and a mixture of red fruit, but you can also use chopped apricots or pitted cherries.

Makes 12 medium-sized muffins

210 g (7^1/2 oz) unsalted butter, creamed
210 g (7^1/2 oz) soft brown sugar
1 tablespoon clear honey
3 eggs, beaten
330 g (11^1/2 oz) plain flour
6 tablespoons unsweetened cocoa powder
10 g (^{1}/4 oz) baking powder
pinch of salt
150 ml (^{1}/4 pint) milk
100 g (3^1/2 oz) chocolate chips
60 g (2^1/4 oz) raspberries
60 g (2^1/4 oz) redcurrants
60 g (2^1/4 oz) blackberries

Preheat the oven to 190°C (375°F), gas mark 5.
Mix the creamed butter with the soft brown sugar and honey in a mixing bowl. Add the eggs, flour, baking powder, cocoa and salt.
Mixing briskly, gradually add the milk and then the chocolate chips.
Butter a 12-space muffin tin or line with paper baking cases. Two-thirds fill the spaces (or baking cases) with muffin mixture and top with the fruit, pushing it lightly into the mixture.
Cook in the preheated oven for 22–25 minutes. Allow to cool a little before removing the muffins from the pan to a wire rack, or serve warm. (If using baking cases, leave the muffins in the cases.)

Chocolate apple crumble

This chocolate crumble might be easy to make but it is nonetheless delicious, especially when served warm with a scoop of vanilla or cinnamon ice cream, or a spoonful of crème fraîche. In season, you can add fresh raspberries to the apples or replace them with a mixture of red fruit.

Serves 6

CHOCOLATE CRUMBLE
2 tablespoons unsweetened cocoa powder
35 g (1¼ oz) dark chocolate chips
135 g (4¾ oz) plain flour
100 g (3½ oz) unsalted butter
80 g (2¾ oz) soft light brown sugar
1 teaspoon ground cinnamon
pinch of salt

Put all the ingredients in a mixing bowl and rub lightly with your fingertips until you have a coarse, crumbly texture. Chill in the refrigerator.

APPLE FILLING
2 tablespoons dark rum
60 g (2¼ oz) raisins
1 kg (2 lb 4 oz) apples
3 tablespoons unsalted butter
3 tablespoons caster sugar
1 teaspoon ground cinnamon

Warm the rum, add the raisins, and leave to soak. Peel and core the apples and cut into thin slices. Melt the butter in a frying pan and lightly brown the apples for 7–8 minutes, adding the sugar and cinnamon after 3–4 minutes and then the raisins and rum.

TO ASSEMBLE AND BAKE THE CRUMBLE
icing sugar

Heat the oven to 200°C (400°F), gas mark 6.
Half-fill an ovenproof dish or 6 individual earthenware dishes with the apple filling. Cover with the chocolate crumble mixture and cook in the preheated oven for 20–25 minutes.
Dust with icing sugar just before serving.

Chocolate and pistachio financiers

These small, oval or rectangular sponge cakes, made with finely ground almonds and egg whites, are delicious served with afternoon tea or with coffee at the end of a meal. Large cakes can also be made with the same mixture and are traditionally decorated with flaked almonds and crystallized fruit. When making small financiers, use silicon moulds – they do not need to be buttered and floured, and it is much easier to turn out the cakes.

Makes 20 financiers

BASIC SPONGE MIXTURE
300 g (10^{1}/2 oz) unsalted butter
10 egg whites, at room temperature
170 g (6 oz) ground almonds
320 g (11^{1}/2 oz) icing sugar
100 g (3^{1}/2 oz) plain flour

Heat the butter in a pan until it acquires a light nut-brown colour then pass through a fine-mesh sieve.
In a separate bowl gradually incorporate the egg whites into the dry ingredients with a wooden spoon. Carefully add the melted butter, stirring continuously, until you obtain a smooth, even texture. Divide the mixture into two bowls, placing two-thirds in one bowl and one-third in the other.

CHOCOLATE-FLAVOURED SPONGE
3 tablespoons unsweetened cocoa powder
^{2}/3 of the basic sponge mixture

Add the cocoa to the sponge mixture and mix well in.

PISTACHIO-FLAVOURED SPONGE
35 g (1^{1}/4 oz) pistachio paste
^{1}/3 of the basic sponge mixture

Add the pistachio paste to the sponge mixture and mix well in.

TO MAKE THE FINANACIERS
Preheat the oven to 200°C (400°F), gas mark 6.
Butter 20 financier moulds 9 cm/3^{1}/2 inches long by 4 cm/1^{1}/2 inches wide and 2.5 cm/1 inch deep. (Alternatively butter 10 moulds and bake the financiers in two batches.)
Divide the two sponge mixtures between the moulds, adding twice as much chocolate as pistachio.
Lightly swirl the two flavours together with a teaspoon to create a marbled effect.
Bake in the preheated oven for 15–20 minutes.
Turn the financiers out of the moulds as soon as they are removed from the oven, and leave to cool on a wire cake rack.

Chocolate orange Breton sablé

This Breton sablé tart tastes just as good as it looks and will certainly impress your guests. Its contrasting textures – the creamy smoothness of the confectioners' custard and crunchiness of the sablé, highlighted by the freshness of the oranges – combine to create a particularly interesting dessert. Serve with a Gewürztraminer Vendange Tardive, a late-harvest wine from Alsace, for an even more enjoyable experience.

Serves 6

RICH SHORTCRUST PASTRY
3 egg yolks
100 g (3¹/2 oz) caster sugar
150 g (5 oz) plain flour
2 teaspoons baking powder
pinch of salt
100 g (3¹/2 oz) unsalted butter, creamed

Preheat the oven to 160°C (325°F), gas mark 3.
Beat the egg yolks and sugar with an electric whisk.
Sift the flour, baking powder and salt.
When the eggs are well beaten, add the creamed butter and sifted flour mixture. Mix to obtain a smooth evenly textured dough, but do not overwork the pastry.
Chill in the refrigerator for 3 hours. Butter a 22-cm/8¹/2-inch flan ring and place on a baking sheet
Roll the pastry out into a circle about 6 mm/¹/4 inch thick and line the flan ring. Prick the base with a fork.
Bake in the preheated oven for 25–30 minutes. Remove from the flan ring and leave to cool on a wire rack.

CHOCOLATE CONFECTIONERS' CUSTARD
50 g (1³/4 oz) best quality dark chocolate, 70% cocoa solids
250 g (9 oz) confectioners' custard (see recipe p. 20)
1¹/2 tablespoons whipping cream

Melt the chocolate in a microwave, following the maker's instructions, or in a bowl set over a pan of barely simmering water (the bowl must not touch the water). Warm the confectioners' custard and stir in the melted chocolate. Add the whipping cream and mix well to obtain a smooth, even texture. Spread evenly over the sablé base.

TO ASSEMBLE THE TART
6 oranges
candied orange peel
chocolate shavings
icing sugar

Peel the oranges and remove the pith. Then, using a small knife, separate the segments and remove the membrane.
Arrange the orange segments in concentric circles over the layer of confectioners' custard. Decorate with a few pieces of candied orange peel and chocolate shavings. Finish with a dusting of icing sugar around the edge of the sablé, forming a border about 0.5 cm/¹/4 inch wide. If you prefer, you can make 6 individual sablés rather than one large one.

Gluttony

As evening falls and the ticking of the clock echoes more loudly in the gathering darkness of the house, the old woman becomes a little girl again. She rummages in her old oak cupboard, one of those antique wardrobes that smell deliciously of herbal tea, beeswax and white bread. Her hand trembles with anticipation, she hesitates, chooses a chocolate, replaces it, chooses another… She can't decide which one to share with her little dog. 'Shall we have a chocolate praline?' The animal pricks up its ears in its basket. But they do not stop at one – or even two – and, one by one, the chocolates disappear.

'Lord! Who has not eaten a little more than is strictly necessary?'
(Saint Augustin)

Chocolate spice cake
(*pain d'épices*)

Although generally regarded as the French equivalent of gingerbread, *pain d'épices* (literally 'spice bread') is a cake made from flour, honey and spices and does not necessarily contain ginger. The mixed spice used in this recipe is widely available in shops and supermarkets but you can personalize your cake by mixing your own spices. All you need is a little ground cinnamon, cloves, cardamom and ginger. Serve with an old Armagnac or Cognac to bring out the flavour of the spices.

Serves 8

220 g (8 oz) all-flower honey
220 g (8 oz) plain flour
60 g (2¼ oz) rye flour
4½ tablespoons unsweetened cocoa powder
2 teaspoons baking powder
2 teaspoons mixed spice
85 g (3 oz) soft dark brown sugar
1 egg
100 ml (3½ fl oz) milk
65 g (2¼ oz) unsalted butter, creamed

Preheat the oven to 180°C (350°F), gas mark 4.
Bring the honey to the boil, remove from the heat and leave until lukewarm. Sift the two flours, cocoa, baking powder and mixed spice into a bowl. In a separate, larger bowl, beat the egg and sugar with a balloon whisk, add the milk and creamed butter, and then the warm honey. Stir in the sifted ingredients and mix well to obtain a smooth, even texture.
Butter and flour a 20-cm/8-inches square baking tin, or a 500-g (1-lb) loaf tin. You can vary the shape of your spice cake by using differently shaped tins. Bake in the preheated oven for about 45 minutes.
Turn out of the baking tin immediately and leave to cool on a wire rack.

Chocolate and hazelnut croquettes

Sweet croquettes are small, crunchy petit-four biscuits that come in various shapes – diamonds, rectangles or rounds – and go wonderfully well with tea or coffee. If you prefer, you can replace the hazelnuts with almonds.

Makes 40–50 croquettes

3 tablespoons unsweetened cocoa powder
90 g (3^1/4 oz) whole hazelnuts
185 g (6^1/2 oz) unsalted butter
235 g (8^1/2 oz) plain flour
95 g (3^1/4 oz) icing sugar
1 egg
pinch of salt

Heat the oven to 190°C (375°F), gas mark 5.
Place the hazelnuts in a baking tin and toast in the preheated oven for 8–10 minutes. Leave to cool. Rub the nuts together to remove the skins, then crush lightly.
Rub the butter into the flour with your fingertips until you have a light, crumbly mixture. Add the icing sugar and cocoa, then the egg and salt. Mix to obtain a smooth, evenly textured dough, but do not overwork. Then add the crushed hazelnuts, mixing well in.
Shape the dough into sausage shapes about 3 cm/ 1^1/4 inches in diameter and chill in the refrigerator for around 4 hours.
When ready to bake the croquettes, preheat the oven to 180°C (350°F), gas mark 4.
Cut the 'sausages' into rounds about 5 mm/^{1}/4 inch thick and place on a baking sheet lined with nonstick baking parchment.
Bake in the preheated oven for 15–20 minutes.

Charlotte

Most of us can remember enjoying a helping of charlotte on some special occasion. It is a firm favourite with all age groups. However, if it is going to be eaten by children you may want to reduce the amount of rum! It is even more delicious served as a dessert with crème anglaise custard, or a swirl of whipped cream.

Serves 6

190 g (6³/4 oz) best quality dark chocolate, 70% cocoa solids
115 g (4 oz) unsalted butter, cut into small pieces
3 egg yolks + 4 egg whites
5¹/2 tablespoons caster sugar
100 ml (3¹/2 fl oz) water
100 ml (3¹/2 fl oz) dark rum
25 sponge finger biscuits (boudoir biscuits or ladyfingers)

Peel off a few chocolate shavings from the chocolate bar with a vegetable peeler and set aside for decoration. Melt the chocolate in a microwave, following the maker's instructions, or in a bowl set over a pan of barely simmering water (the bowl must not touch the water). Remove from the heat and add the butter, whisking to obtain a smooth texture, then carefully incorporate the egg yolks.

Beat the egg whites until they form stiff peaks, adding half the sugar about halfway through. Then carefully incorporate the egg whites into the chocolate-and-egg mixture using a metal spoon. Mix the water, rum and rest of the sugar in a basin, and dip the sponge fingers quickly, just sufficiently long enough for them to take on a colour.
Line the base and sides of a 16-cm/6¹/4-inch charlotte mould with the sponge fingers, so that the rounded side of each biscuit faces outward.
Pour the chocolate mousse into the mould and cover with the remaining sponge fingers.
Chill in the refrigerator for 4 hours.
Remove the charlotte from the mould by turning out onto a serving plate. If it refuses to move, dip the mould for a few seconds in a basin of hot water.
Decorate with chocolate shavings.

Chocolate-chip brioches

Brioches are one of the most popular pastries in France and come in various forms, depending on the region. The brioches in this recipe can be eaten for breakfast or a snack and are even more delicious served warm with a cup of creamy hot chocolate. Or for something a little different, they can be sliced and dipped in a mixture of beaten egg yolk and milk, then fried and sprinkled with sugar.

Makes 2 x 350 g (12 oz) brioches

250 g (9 oz) plain flour
2 tablespoons caster sugar
pinch of salt
2 x 7 g (¼ oz) sachets dried yeast
3 eggs
185 g (6¼ oz) unsalted butter, cut into small pieces
80 g (3 oz) chocolate chips
2 tablespoons glaze (see recipe p. 62)

Put the flour, sugar, salt, yeast and eggs into a food processor fitted with the hook attachment and mix for about 10 minutes at medium speed. When the dough begins to come away from the sides of the bowl, add the butter and continue mixing until it is well worked in and the dough begins to come away from the sides again. Add the chocolate chips and mix carefully. Leave the dough in the bowl of the processor, cover with clingfilm or a clean cloth, and leave to stand for 1½–2 hours in a warm place until the dough has doubled in volume.

Butter two rectangular cake tins 18 cm/7 inches long by 9 cm/3½ inches deep (or two brioche moulds). On a floured work surface, knead the dough rapidly by hand so that it returns to its original volume and then divide into 8 balls. Gently pull each ball into a slightly oval shape and then place 4 ovals upright in each tin or brioche mould.
Leave to stand at room temperature until the dough is level with the edges of the tin and the ovals have expanded and merged.
Preheat the oven to 200°C (400°F), gas mark 6.
Glaze the brioches and make a few small incisions in the surface of each ball using wet scissors.
Bake in the preheated oven for 25–30 minutes. Remove from the moulds and leave to cool slightly.

Cookies

These cookies can be flavoured with a variety of ingredients – pecan or macadamia nuts, candied orange peel, hazelnuts, raisins, or chocolate chips – that will delight all lovers of cakes and pastries. Cookies can be enjoyed at any time of the day and are even more delicious when they are warm and slightly soft in the centre.

Makes about 30 cookies

100 g (3$^{1}/_{2}$ oz) unsalted butter
100 g (3$^{1}/_{2}$ oz) slightly salted butter
140 g (5 oz) icing sugar
200 g (7 oz) soft dark brown sugar
400 g (14 oz) plain flour
1 teaspoon bicarbonate soda (optional)
2 eggs
300 g (10$^{1}/_{2}$ oz) best quality dark chocolate, 70% cocoa solids
200 g (7 oz) whole blanched almonds
200 g (7 oz) walnuts

Preheat the oven to 180°C (350°F), gas mark 4. Warm both types of butter and mix together with the icing sugar and brown sugar. Add the flour and bicarbonate of soda (if used), and then incorporate the eggs.

Chop the chocolate and roughly chop the almonds and walnuts using a knife or food processor, then add to the mixture.

Shape the dough into regularly shaped 'sausages' about 5 cm/2 inches in diameter and chill in the refrigerator for 2 hours. Cut the dough into slices about 1 cm/$^{1}/_{2}$ inch thick and place on a baking sheet lined with nonstick baking parchment.

Bake in the preheated oven for 20–25 minutes. Remove from the baking sheet and leave to cool on a wire rack. To keep the cookies crisp, store in an airtight container.

Brownies

The secret of success when making these traditional cakes from the United States is to cook them for exactly the right amount of time. If they are overcooked, they dry out and lose their soft, melting texture – they should be only just cooked in the centre. They are delicious warm, either on their own or with a scoop of vanilla ice cream or a spoonful of crème fraîche.

Makes 20 brownies

195 g (7 oz) best quality dark chocolate,
70% cocoa solids (USA bittersweet not unsweetened)
345 g (12 oz) unsalted butter, creamed
6 eggs
170 g (6 oz) caster sugar
170 g (6 oz) soft dark brown sugar
170 g (6 oz) plain flour
240 g (8½ oz) chopped walnuts
walnut pieces
icing sugar

Preheat the oven to 180°C (350°F), gas mark 4.
Melt the chocolate in a microwave, following the maker's instructions, or in a bowl set over a pan of barely simmering water (the bowl must not touch the water). Add the butter and stir until you have a smooth texture.
Then incorporate the eggs, caster sugar and brown sugar, the flour and chopped walnuts, mixing well to obtain an evenly textured mixture. Pour into a rectangular baking tin – 36 cm/14½ inches long by 26 cm/10½ inches wide and 2.5 cm/1 inch deep – lined with nonstick baking parchment.
Cook in the preheated oven for 18–20 minutes. Leave to cool and cut into portions. Decorate each brownie with walnut pieces and/or a dusting of icing sugar.

Gâteau de Nany

This recipe makes an ideal birthday cake. Quick and simple to prepare, it can be baked in different types of tins to produce all kinds of shapes, covered with ready-made or homemade icing, and decorated with whatever meets the latest craze – children just love it! But its main attraction is its soft, melting texture.

Serves 6

225 g (8 oz) best quality dark chocolate, 70% cocoa solids
7 eggs
350 g (12 oz) caster sugar
190 g (6¾ oz) unsalted butter, creamed
180 g (6¼ oz) plain flour
icing sugar

Preheat the oven to 180°C (350°F), gas mark 4.
Melt the chocolate in a microwave, following the maker's instructions, or in a bowl set over a pan of barely simmering water (the bowl must not touch the water).
Separate the eggs. Beat the yolks with the sugar until the mixture lightens in colour. Add the creamed butter and melted chocolate, mix well and then gradually incorporate the flour.
Using an electric whisk, beat the egg whites until they form stiff peaks, then incorporate carefully into the chocolate-and-egg mixture.
Butter and flour a 26-cm/10½-inch cake tin, pour in the cake mixture and cook in the preheated oven for 40–45 minutes. Leave to cool before removing from the tin. Decorate with a simple dusting of icing sugar or more elaborately for those extra special occasions.

Index of recipes

The secrets of
Lionel Lallement

Lionel Lallement was never in any doubt about his chosen career and, at the age of 15, embarked upon an apprenticeship leading to a vocational training certificate that qualified him as a baker and pastrycook. He went on to win a number of professional awards, including the Prix des Entremets Petit-Four and the Pièce Artistique gastronomy award. In 1989, he was awarded the Meilleur Ouvrier de France (MOF) – Best Craftsmen in France – in the pastry and confectionery division and, at the age of 24, became chef for Saint-Clair le Traiteur. He has remained loyal to the famous Parisian caterer and delicatessen and every season produces a unique selection of pastries and confectionery that combines creativity and innovation.

PERCENTAGES IN CHOCOLATE

For some time, chocolate manufacturers have prided themselves on the fact that the percentage of cocoa solids in their products is shown on the packaging. In fact the practice has become something of a marketing ploy, and people are taken in by it.

When manufacturers indicate a certain percentage of cocoa solids, say 60% or 75%, on a bar of chocolate, they are in fact suggesting and leading consumers to believe that the higher the percentage, the better the chocolate. This is simply not true. The percentage of cocoa solids shown on a bar of chocolate is the sum total of the cocoa powder and cocoa butter contained in the bar.

For example, let's compare two bars of dark chocolate, one with 71% cocoa solids, the other with 66%. In the first instance, the actual composition of the chocolate is:
• 45% cocoa butter,
• 26% cocoa powder (for 71%),
• 29% sugar.
In the second, the actual composition is:
• 36% cocoa butter,
• 30% cocoa powder (for 66%),
• 34% sugar.

So it can be seen that the chocolate with 71% cocoa solids in fact contains less cocoa powder and more cocoa butter than the chocolate with 66%, and that the second bar of chocolate contains more sugar than the first. The cocoa butter primarily affects the texture and hardness of the chocolate – its effect on the flavour is incidental. The cocoa powder gives the chocolate its characteristics – acidity, bitterness, aroma, fruitiness, toasted quality, potassium content, etc. It can therefore be deduced that the percentage of cocoa solids is not an indicator of the quality of the chocolate, but only a part of its composition, which is often far from precise.

A WORD OF ADVICE
Consult an artisan chocolatier and listen to his advice and what he has to say about the origins of the chocolate he suggests. Just like a sommelier selecting a good-quality wine, the chocolatier will find you the chocolate of your dreams.

KEEPING CHOCOLATE FRESH

As everyone knows, chocolate is a fragile product that not only reacts with heat but also with air.

This is why most bars of good-quality chocolate sold in shops and supermarkets are first of all wrapped in foil to protect them from the heat, and then in a cardboard sleeve to protect them from the air and variations in temperature.

Exposed to the air, chocolate will automatically dry out, lose its aroma, its melting texture and its flavour. Remember that the flavours of chocolate are volatile and the less well protected it is, the more it loses its flavour. This is demonstrated by the fact that when you first open a box of chocolates, there is a very strong aroma.

This is why it is so important to buy freshly prepared chocolate. A good example of this is Easter – every year, chocolate rabbits and Easter eggs appear earlier and earlier on the supermarket shelves. An artisan chocolatier, on the other hand, will melt his chocolate at the last possible moment, pouring and assembling his creations as near as possible to the actual date in order to maximize their quality. If you go into a shop that sells hand-made chocolates you will always be greeted by the delicious aroma resulting from the volatile flavours of freshly poured chocolate.

A WORD OF ADVICE
Buy your chocolate from an artisan chocolatier, freshly poured and made – the quality will be as good as it gets.

Keep chocolate in a dry place (16–18°C/61–64°F), wrapped in clingfilm and stored in an airtight container to protect it from the air and humidity.

The secrets of Thierry Mulhaupt

Thierry Mulhaupt trained in Paris, working with some of France's greatest pastrycooks during the day and studying at the city's famous art college, the École des Beaux-Arts, in the evening. He won the Prix Jean-Louis-Berthelot in Paris, and first prize at the Olympiades de la Gastronomie in Frankfurt. His patisserie is conceived like a work of art in which flavours and decorations are composed with elegance and precision. He settled in the historic centre of Strasbourg in 1991 and, in 1999, opened a shop specializing in *pain d'épices* ('spice bread') and chocolates.

A GUIDE TO TASTING

I would like to try and describe a few key elements that will enable you to experience the maximum amount of sensations when tasting a chocolate. We have five senses at our disposal, and each can help us to make discoveries that are as wonderful as they are amazing.

Sight: start by considering the appearance of a chocolate. If it is light in colour, it will contain less cocoa, if it is dark, it will contain more – the shades of light and dark vary according to the origin of the cocoa beans. You can also consider how shiny it is – a sign that it has kept well and also of the quality of the chocolate-making process.

Touch: a chocolate should be smooth, soft and silky to the touch. Touch should be an integral part of tasting.

Hearing: plays a very small part in tasting, but when you break a bar of chocolate, there's a pleasant little snapping sound. If it is high pitched, it means that the chocolate has a high cocoa content or is relatively cold (and therefore too cold for tasting) – the ideal temperature is 20–21°C/68–70°F. If it is low pitched and dull, it means that the bar has a low cocoa content or that the temperature is too high.

Smell: when tasting chocolate, you can refer to the 'nose' just as you would for wine. Before putting a chocolate in your mouth, hold it to your nose and inhale gently. This gives you an idea of the dominant aromas of cocoa, and secondary aromas such as spices, wood, toasted or earthy qualities, tobacco, leather and even, for a certain variety of cocoa, petroleum.

Taste: when you taste chocolate, it's important to chew it well. It has to melt in your mouth to release all the flavours. At this stage, we refer to flavours, since what you taste corresponds to three of the four existing flavours – sweet, bitter and tart. You'll always find these three flavours in chocolate, but in different proportions depending on the cocoa content and origin of the beans.

When you swallow the chocolate, the aromatic notes are confirmed by what is known as retro-olfaction – air exhaled through the nose. As for wine, you can refer to length on the palate or persistence in the mouth. The best type of chocolate should be long on the palate and have a good aftertaste. Just like wine, this can be measured in caudalies (a unit for quantifying persistence in the mouth of the flavours after tasting).

A good-quality chocolate should have a story to tell. It should have a good aromatic palette, be shiny, tasty, full of flavour and, above all, have a good length on the palate. Occasionally I don't use any of the above criteria, but wolf down a bar simply because I feel like it. That's another thing about chocolate – you can enjoy it in any number of different ways.

A FEW TASTING SUGGESTIONS

One final word of advice, enjoy your chocolate with a glass of wine, a liqueur or even a cigar for that complete chocolate experience.

Chocolate éclair	A good-quality mocha coffee
Dark chocolate 70% cocoa solids	Lapsang Souchong, a broad-leaved tea with a smoky taste and aroma
Dark chocolate 60% cocoa solids	A Criolos chocolate-flavoured beer (brewed in Alsace with cocoa beans – with an aroma and aftertaste of chocolate) and a Vegas Robaina Unicos (Cuban) cigar
Chocolate orange cake	Gewürztraminer 1989 (Jossmeyer SGN, Alsace)
Dark chocolate mousse with raspberries	Domaine de la Grange des Pères 1999 (Languedoc)
Chocolate tartlets	Noir de Grenache (Domaine des Mille Vignes, Fitou)
Dark chocolate 85% cocoa solids	An old rum and a Partagas Lusitania (Cuban) cigar

The secrets of
Henri Le Roux

The son of a Breton pastrycook who lived and worked in the United States, Australia and France, Henri Le Roux was brought up in the world of cakes and pastries. After training in Switzerland, he settled in the French fishing port of Quiberon, Brittany, where he opened a workshop and shop selling hand-made confectionery and patisserie in 1977. His top-secret caramel and chocolate recipes brought him immediate success. Every year, the creator of caramel made with salted butter – *caramel au beurre salé* or CBS in French – adds other wonderful innovations to his repertoire, for example the dark-chocolate egg (Chítou) filled with a soft caramel made with butter and Belgian beer.

GANACHE

Ganache is an extremely delicate, creamy preparation with a melting texture made from chocolate and cream. It is used as a topping, filling, coating or decoration for large and small cakes, sweets and chocolate desserts. There are any number of ganache recipes whose main difference lies in the choice of flavouring.

But how is it that a ganache prepared under the same conditions, with the same ingredients and according to the same recipe, can have a different consistency each time you make it? At the first attempt, you may produce a perfect ganache with a melting texture that is easy to serve, whereas the next time you are faced with a disappointing creation that is too soft and therefore difficult to handle.

To ensure consistent results each time, always pour the mixture into the pastry case or mould at exactly the same temperature, i.e. 31–32°C/88–90°F. Then cover with clingfilm and leave for 12 hours before serving.

A FEW WORDS OF ADVICE WHEN
MAKING A GANACHE
Choosing the chocolate: the type of chocolate depends on how firm you want the ganache to be. Always choose a chocolate with a higher proportion of cocoa powder and a lower proportion of cocoa butter. The cocoa powder contains the chocolate flavours, while the cocoa butter (which is white and is also used to make white chocolate) merely enriches and improves the consistency.

Confectioners' chocolate: as its name suggests, this chocolate is used for coating confectionery and cakes. Be careful if using confectioners' chocolate to make a ganache as it contains a higher percentage of cocoa butter – it consequently has very little taste and makes the ganache harder and fattier than it should be. It is the cocoa powder that contains all the delicate aromas of the chocolate, so if you do use confectioners' chocolate to make a ganache, you need to allow a larger amount of chocolate to obtain the same results.

WHITE CHOCOLATE

White chocolate only contains one component of chocolate – cocoa butter. It is a creamy white colour and has little or no taste since it doesn't contain the other component, the dark brown cocoa powder that contains all the flavours of the chocolate. Strictly speaking, because it lacks the principal component, white 'chocolate' shouldn't really be classified as a chocolate.

The secrets of
Pierre Marcolini

Pierre Marcolini is a young Belgian chocolatier who has gone from strength to strength and gained international renown. He has been passionate about chocolate since his childhood and won some of the most prestigious international awards, becoming World Pastry Champion in Lyon, in 1995, and European Pastry Champion, in 2000. To this passion for his chosen profession, Pierre Marcolini adds his own brand of creativity that has given rise to such innovations as cinnamon chocolates and petit-four biscuits with mountain honey or tonka beans.

HOW TO MAKE A REALLY GOOD HOT CHOCOLATE

A traditional hot chocolate is made with 600 ml/1 pint milk to 250 g/9 oz chocolate. Choose best quality dark (bittersweet) chocolate, with about 70% cocoa solids, made with Venezuelan cocoa (Caracas cacao).

Chop the chocolate finely with a knife or vegetable chopper to obtain fine shavings. Bring the milk to the boil with a vanilla pod, split open, or cinnamon stick, then remove and pour the milk gradually onto the chocolate shavings. Add the milk to the chocolate in several goes, taking the time to whisk the mixture gently so that the shavings melt gradually.

DIFFERENCES IN TASTE BETWEEN DIFFERENT GROWTHS

Just as wine is classified according to growths (crus), each botanical variety of cocoa produces a specific growth, according to the conditions under which it is cultivated.

Criollo: a Mexican cocoa (cocoa of the Mayas), is the rarest and most delicate variety, representing less than 5% of world production. It has a heavily scented, fruity flavour and a subtle aroma that varies from region to region and from year to year.

Forastero: a cocoa from Upper Amazonia, is much hardier and has a fuller, more pronounced flavour. Cultivated in Africa, it produces fairly ordinary growths, but in Ecuador and Venezuela, the Equatorial climate gives it an incredible fineness.

Trinitario: a hybrid descended from a cross between Criollo and Forastero, is cultivated in South America and Indonesia, with the best growths coming from Trinidad and Java. It has a fruity flavour and a good length on the palate.

Each variety has its own specific gustatory characteristics that are enhanced by a favourable climate and a relatively rich soil.

MAKING DARK, MILK, AND WHITE CHOCOLATE

Each of these three types of chocolate is obtained by means of the same process – the cocoa beans are cleaned, dried, crushed and roasted, then ground in mills to obtain cocoa paste (chocolate liquor).

The paste is then pressed to remove the natural fatty material (cocoa butter), leaving the cocoa cake (cocoa paste with most of the fat removed) that is ground to make cocoa powder.

Dark chocolate and milk chocolate are both made from a blend of cocoa butter and cocoa powder.

Dark chocolate is made by adding a little sugar, vanilla and soya lecithin. Milk chocolate has a lower cocoa content (around 30%) than dark chocolate and milk powder is added to give it its characteristic sweetness and smooth, creamy texture. White chocolate, on the other hand, is made by adding sugar and milk to the cocoa butter pressed out of the cocoa paste. It is the cocoa butter that gives the 'chocolate' its white colour. For this reason, certain purists don't regard it as a 'proper' chocolate, but as a piece of confectionery made from cocoa butter.

The secrets of André Cordel

André Cordel was born in Verdun, northeastern France, and grew up in his father's baker's shop where he gained a vocational training certificate that qualified him as a baker and pastrycook. In the 1970s he studied at the famous Coba school in Basle, Switzerland and the École Lenôtre in Paris. He went on to practise his art at the Palet d'Or in Bar-le-Duc (Lorraine) and was acclaimed one of the great master patissiers by the Club des Croqueurs de Chocolat (Chocolate Crunchers' Club) and the Association of the Relais Desserts International. His imaginative chocolate creations include Bâtons des Maréchaux (marshals' batons), Renaissance and Symphonie, a chocolate dessert that won first prize in the French National Pastry Championship.

ICED DESSERTS

An ice cream or sorbet is always a popular dessert, but it can be very disappointing when you serve your guests a scoop of ice cream that melts very quickly and ends up sliding across the plate. A trick of the trade that will help to avoid such problems is to put your plates in the freezer for a few minutes before serving the dessert. In this way, they'll be cold enough to stop it melting before it is eaten, and your iced desserts will be as good to look at as they are to eat.

CHOCOLATE MOUSSE

There are a few basic rules for making a successful chocolate mousse. Always use good-quality chocolate and exact quantities, and make sure the whipped cream is firm – but this is often difficult to achieve as the mixture of melted chocolate and cream slackens very quickly, even when mixed with the greatest care. The trick is to pour the chocolate and about 10% of the whipped cream into a bowl, cover with clingfilm and bring to the boil in the microwave. Remove the mixture and leave to stand until it cools to a temperature of about 35–37°C/95–99°F. Then you can gently incorporate the rest of the whipped cream. Served at room temperature, your mousse will be creamy and firm, but not fragile.

SALT YOUR DESSERTS

Add character to hot-chocolate and melted-chocolate desserts with a tiny pinch of salt. You'll be amazed by the result!

ADD CHOCOLATE TO SAVOURY SAUCES

Preparing a sauce with red wine or a marinade to accompany game is not always that simple. Adding a small amount of a very flavourful chocolate or, even better still, cocoa paste (chocolate liquor) not only helps to bind the sauce but also makes the cooked wine a little less bitter. Leave to simmer for a long time to obtain a sauce that is extremely dark, shiny and exceptionally smooth.

The secrets of
Sébastien Gaudard

Sébastien Gaudard grew up in his parents' patisserie and has worked and trained with a number of great pastry chefs. He served his apprenticeship with Georges Vergne in the Territoire de Belfort, a tiny department on the Franco-Swiss border, and then worked for two years with Gérard Banwarth at the Pâtisserie Jacques in Mulhouse. He spent eight years as pastry chef at Fauchon, the famous Parisian caterer and delicatessen, before working for three years as sous-chef to Pierre Hermé. On November 1, 2001, he founded a consultancy for patissiers-restaurateurs and, in 2003, opened Delicabar – the first Snack Chic – in the Bon Marché department store in Paris.

FLAVOURING A GANACHE

Ganache is used for assembling macaroons, filling petits fours, truffles, chocolates and cakes. It can be firm, thick, creamy and even runny (chocolate sauce). It is a mixture of fatty materials contained in the chocolate, and water contained in the cream, milk and even the crushed fruit used to flavour it. It is the result of an emulsion that is very similar to the principle of making a mayonnaise.

The procedure for making a ganache remains the same whatever ingredients are added (honey, spices, pears, etc.).

To flavour a ganache, start by chopping the chocolate into small pieces. Put the required quantity of milk or a mixture of milk and double cream in a pan with the spices of your choice – Darjeeling tea (2–3 teabags), Tahitian vanilla (2 pods) or cinnamon (3 sticks) – and bring to the boil. Remove from the heat and leave to infuse for 3–15 minutes, depending on the required strength of the flavouring. Check the intensity of flavour before passing the liquid through a fine-mesh sieve – you should end up with the original amount of liquid (make up if necessary). Gradually pour the liquid onto the chopped chocolate, stirring with a balloon whisk, until you have a shiny, pliable mixture. Process in an electric blender to perfect the texture.

FOR A SUCCESSFUL CHOCOLATE CHANTILLY CREAM

Here is a quick recipe that can't fail to impress your guests. It is made with 240 ml/8½ fl oz whipping cream (35% fat) and one of the following:
- 160 g/5½ oz milk chocolate, 40% cocoa solids;
- 130 g/4¾ oz confectioners' chocolate, 70% cocoa solids;
- 140 g/5 oz confectioners' chocolate, 64% cocoa solids.

You can also personalize this recipe by infusing the cream with any number of different aromatic ingredients (see 'Flavouring a ganache' in left-hand column).

Three hours before you make the Chantilly cream, put the whipping cream in a pan and add the aromatic ingredient of your choice – for example, Earl Grey tea flavoured with bergamot (2–3 teabags), mixed spice and chestnut honey to taste, ground Java peppercorns to taste, a few fresh mint leaves, or a few basil leaves and grated lime zest. Bring to the boil, remove from the heat and leave to infuse for 3–15 minutes, depending on the required strength of the flavouring. Check the intensity of flavour before passing through a fine-mesh sieve and chilling on the lower shelf of the refrigerator.

When ready to make the Chantilly cream, whip the cream until it is light and frothy. Melt the chopped chocolate in a microwave, following the maker's instructions, or in a bowl set over a pan of barely simmering water (the bowl must not touch the water). Add a quarter of the whipped cream and mix until you obtain a consistency similar to that of the cream. Reheat if necessary, then add the rest of the whipped cream. Finally, enjoy this smooth, shiny chocolate Chantilly cream with its delicately scented aromas.

The editor's acknowledgements

The editor would like to thank the following stores for their kind collaboration:
Agapé: p. 32, 34, 36, 52, 60, 78, 84, 86, 92, 94, 100, 106, 112 / Anna Médeiros: p. 62 / Astier de Villatte: p. 8, 12, 18, 28, 32, 58, 96, 114 / Créations Mathias: p. 10, 30, 52, 74, 96 / Coquet: p. 44, 62 / Côté bastide: p. 26, 42, 44, 78, 84 / Cristal Saint-Louis: p. 24, 114 / Deyrolle: p. 6, 46 / Farfelus Farfadets: p. 10, 12, 18, 28, 56, 62, 66, 80, 94, 96, 116 / Farrow & Ball: p. 24, 32, 50, 52, 70, 78, 86, 94, 96, 114 / Fouquet confiserie: p. 40, 52, 82, 86, 106 / Gaspari: p. 16 /
Mille Feuilles: p. 44, 114 / Mokuba: p. 24, 30, 32, 44, 64, 86, 94, 96, 114 / Nobilis: p. 12, 44, 46, 64, 74, 78, 82, 84, 90, 96, 102, 112 / Pierre Frey: p. 6, 26, 36, 66, 70, 96 / Point à la ligne: p. 12, 18, 44, 78 / Samaritaine: p. 16, 32, 36, 84, 92, 100, 102, 108 / Siècle: p. 60, 70, 84 / Tissage de Luz: p. 24, 86, 118.
Gontran Cherrier for his superb work and active participation in the project
Fabien Rouillard of Création Conseil Dessert (www.ccdessert.com)
for his help in creating and photographing the desserts
Gaëlle Moreno for her invaluable and very effective help

The designer's acknowledgements

Véronique Villaret would like to thank all the really nice press attachées and designers who supported
and encouraged her in the adventure of this first book, and all the willing hands that worked so hard to
make her task more enjoyable
Thomas, a great gourmet and a brilliant photographer
Gontran for so kindly making some really beautiful cakes
Jérémy and Aimery for their assistance, calmness and sense of humour
Gaëlle for her good nature and knowledge of packaging terms
Milou for a last-minute range of coloured confectionery
Anne and Laurent for sharing their private, poetic world over a few sweetmeats
Anne and Pierre-Jean, for having faith in her and without whom she would not have put on those extra
pounds of sheer heaven
And finally Samba for hands dusted with sweet cocoa powder

The photographer's acknowledgements

Thomas Dhellemmes would like to thank his wife, Valérie, who introduced him to indulgence
Véronique Villaret for everything she contributed with her brightly coloured, poetic world
The entire Hachette team, especially Pierre-Jean Furet for his faith and the freedom he gave the
photographic team
Anne la Fay and Gaëlle Moreno for their kindness and attention
His assistants, Aimery Chemin and Jérémy Zenou, two conscientious workers and real comics

Photographic credits

p. 122, 123, 125, 126: DR; p. 124: Lorraine Le Roux; p. 127: Francesca Mantovani.

Hachette Pratique
Director: Stephen Bateman; Editor-in-chief: Pierre-Jean Furet;
Editorial manager: Anne la Fay; Production manager: Gérard Piassale

Production team
Vanessa Blondel, Marie-Luce Nemo
Artistic director: Philippe Hubert

ISBN 10: 1-84430-176-1
ISBN 13: 978-184430-176-8

Printed by Toppan Printing Co., (HK) Ltd.